Kin Thai

John Chantarasak

KIN THAI

Modern Thai Recipes
to Cook at Home

Photography by Maureen M. Evans

Hardie Grant

BOOKS

Contents

Introduction

I was born in Liverpool to a Thai father and an English mother. I would class myself, as I'm sure many will now in this modern-day Britain, as mixed race. A melting pot of different cultures, distilled into a unique individual. When I was an infant, we relocated as a family to the picturesque Wye Valley in Wales. This is where I remained throughout my childhood, before settling in London in my early twenties. I've been fortunate in that travel was always a large part of my childhood, and this has continued into my adult life. I've travelled and cooked across numerous continents, countries and cities, each time building my experiences, learning about and discovering countless new ingredients and cooking techniques, and forging bonds with a rich diversity of people.

Thailand has always featured in my life. When I was a child, we would travel to Bangkok to visit family and stay at my father's childhood home, in the neighbourhood of Thong-Lor. When my family first bought land and built their home there, it was an area dominated by rice paddy fields servicing the central hub of Bangkok. Now, Thong-Lor is a bustling, modern neighbourhood with prime real estate, trendy restaurants, buzzy bars and a large multicultural population. It's unrecognisable from the land my grandparents, father and aunts grew up on. This is the story of Bangkok in the past century, a city that never sleeps and continues to modernise and grow, day by day.

I've always loved visiting my family and friends in Bangkok. I have fond memories of eating my grandmother's cooking at the family house surrounded by my cousins, aunts and uncles. Everyone would chat away while plate after plate of amazing food was brought out to the table, with vibrant, inviting colours and wonderful aromas. Very often, I would know nothing about the dishes I was spooning into my mouth or what all the different ingredients were dancing across my tongue. I loved the mysterious nature of it all: exotic flavours that felt like the dial was turned up to eleven, sometimes almost unbearably spicy; savoury dishes with a sweetness you might normally associate with a dessert. It was truly bonkers to a curious child. We would frequently visit favourite family restaurants on these trips, often travelling hours by car just to have lunch at a specific seaside location or rural shack specialising in certain dishes – not uncommon behaviour for Thai families, who cherish and value the food they eat. To this day, though, my favourite memories are of my grandmother's food. She was a wonderful cook and the flavours weren't solely Thai, but also nodded to our family's distant roots in China.

My Thai family are the sort of people that wake up to a breakfast spread of broken rice porridge (*jok*) with various toppings, along with some leftovers from the previous night's banquet and plenty of fresh fruits and vegetables. We would only be a few minutes into eating breakfast before someone would ask where we should go or what we should have for lunch, and, more importantly, 'What's for dinner tonight?' Food is everything to Thai people; it's what they live and breathe on a daily basis, and this mentality influenced me more than I could ever have imagined as I was growing up.

In the late summer of 2013, I decided it was time to relocate to Bangkok in Thailand. This was a culmination of various life choices that had seen me leave my London office job and uproot myself from the city at the beginning of that year, before embarking on a bucket list-style road trip across the USA. During that twelve-thousand-mile, country-crossing journey of discovery, I found myself travelling, sometimes for days, to eat at certain restaurants or visit farms that I had read about. It struck me that my love for food and drink may extend further than just a hobby and that hospitality might actually be the industry I was destined for. Around this time, a chance conversation with a Thai friend brought to my attention the recently opened Le Cordon Bleu cooking school at the Dusit Thani Hotel in Bangkok. One thing led to another, and by September of that year I was there, enrolling at my first day of culinary school. Rather remarkably, I studied the Diploma de Cuisine in classical French cookery. It was a revelation: I learned about ingredients, techniques, organisation, hygiene and kitchen hierarchy. I was cooking multiple dishes a day, breaking down animal carcasses, learning to fillet all varieties of fish and working with vegetables I'd never had the confidence to buy at home. I was hooked – and not only that, I also discovered I was quite good at this cooking business. I found myself religiously spending hours in the school library reading cookbooks, practising dishes in my Bangkok apartment and exploring the back alleys and street markets of the city. It was during this time I also started to work in professional kitchens at the weekends and evenings outside of culinary school. To start with, I worked in French and European restaurants, but my interest in Thai food grew as I ate and discovered more about the cuisine, and I soon felt compelled to cook the food of my father's heritage. I was given the opportunity to intern at arguably the most globally recognised Thai restaurant in the country, under the tuition of chefs David Thompson and Prin Polsuk – the world-renowned Nahm. Chef David had already won many accolades at Nahm when it was based in London's Hyde Park Corner, but had

since relocated the restaurant to Bangkok, where it had been recognised as the number-one restaurant in Asia and graced the World Top 50 rankings. It was a wonderful opportunity to learn Thai cuisine from a master of his craft. It was here that my eyes and mind were really opened to Thai cuisine, and, to my shame, I realised very quickly that I knew very little about the food of Thailand and that side of my heritage.

Fortunately, I was now working within a team of dedicated Thai chefs who were eager to share their knowledge and experiences with a naive half-Thai cook who was still struggling to grasp the language and knew relatively little about this exotic cuisine. Time rolled on, and my knowledge and confidence in cooking Thai food grew. It was an exhilarating time: everything was new and fascinating, and I couldn't absorb information fast enough. When not working in the kitchen, I would explore the streets of Bangkok and obsessively read food blogs and forums about Thai food, desperate to know more. The spark had well and truly been ignited. It was a great feeling – I had found my purpose.

After 18 months in Thailand, I had not only learned to cook, but had also found an identity with food. Despite this, I had reached a point where I felt it was time to return to my domestic British home. I'd been away from family, friends and the world I knew for just over two and a half years, with one brief visit back to my homeland to see family. Despite loving this new-found energy and passion for cooking, I was tired from the experience – exhausted in fact. All that moving around and relentless working had drained me of life and I needed to get back to the UK. I told Chef David of my intentions to return home and he was supportive, telling me that if I was not planning to return to Bangkok, then I should reach out to a former employee of his from when Nahm was based in London. That person was Andy Oliver. I met Andy back in London, and we spoke at length about Thai food and people we both knew back in Bangkok. It quickly became apparent we had much in common, and as chance should have it, Andy had been beavering away with supper clubs and events that were gaining attention and momentum. He told me about his concept of old-style Thai food cooked with a blend of Asian and British ingredients – this would become the

respected Thai restaurant Som Saa. I left the meeting curious about how I should approach life back in the UK. Did I plan to stay, or would I be tempted to return to Thailand and continue my education with Chef David at Nahm?

I returned to my childhood home in Wales while I gathered my thoughts and planned my next move. I was keen to continue cooking and increasing my kitchen knowledge, but I wasn't sure if London was the best place to do this. Wales offered a calmer pace of life, a relief from the hustle and bustle of the last few years, refuge from the chaos and a familiar place where I had spent much of my younger life. Within a week, I had written to a number of kitchens and landed work at a restaurant on the outskirts of Bristol called Casamia. It was here that I was first introduced to contemporary British cooking, using different techniques and skills to extract the maximum flavour from a single ingredient, and showcasing these flavours on a seasonal tasting menu. It was fascinating, and the chefs in the kitchen were incredibly transparent with their knowledge, but after a little time I found myself longing for the flavours of Thailand. My pleas were answered by a phone call from Andy. He had secured a location in east London to launch his Som Saa project and was recruiting for the kitchen. I packed my bags and headed back to London to begin the next chapter of my culinary adventures.

The next few years went past in a flash at Som Saa's new home at Climpson's Arch in London Fields. By day, the railway archway was used to roast coffee and package orders for distribution around London, and in the evening we reset the space as a functioning restaurant dining room complete with a bar and outside area where customers could see the chefs cooking over live fires in this rustic yet urban setting. It was chaos and harmony in equal parts. We were cooking for hundreds each evening, armed with little more than charcoal and the punchy flavours of Northeastern Thailand. We were a first for the London food scene, ripping up the rule book, cooking by instinct and with a passion to share the incredibly flavourful and colourful Thai food we knew and loved. Our menu was full of intrigue and was a real departure for those who had previously only had green curry and *pad thai* as their reference point for Thai food in the UK. We served shaved green papaya

salads *(som tam)* dressed with sweet palm sugar, funky fermented fish sauce and ferociously hot chillies; grilled pork neck *(mu yang)* slathered in spicy sauces, herbs and citrus; braised pork belly curry flavoured with dry spices from Burma *(gaeng hung lae)* and served with pickled garlic and fresh ginger; and whole deep-fried sea bass adorned with lemongrass, lime leaves and toasted rice powder. It was food that got the heart thumping and exhilarated the taste buds, and I loved cooking and serving it. Som Saa went from strength to strength, with queues of customers each day and acclaim from the London press. This led to a successful crowdfunding campaign, raising capital to build a bricks-and-mortar site in London's historic Spitalfields. Under the guidance of head chefs Andy and Mark, I climbed the ranks and helped lead the kitchen for the next three years at this restaurant site. During this time, I grew not only as a chef, but as a person. My knowledge of Thai food blossomed and I started to experiment with my own style of cooking.

I found myself more and more curious about the relationship British ingredients could have with Thai cuisine. I loved cooking with the exotic ingredients native to Thailand, but I soon realised that some of the indigenous foods found within the British Isles mirrored the flavour profiles of those found in Asia. This idea really struck home when I came to cook at my first collaborative guest chef event with my now great friend Nicholas Balfe, at his seasonal British restaurant Salon. Nicholas cooks using local – and often hyper-seasonal – ingredients from the British larder. He challenged me to think about substituting Asian ingredients with those that were indigenous to Britain but could still provide the same flavour profile. It was revolutionary to me. We were interchanging core Thai ingredients with British foods, and, to my surprise, the flavours married wonderfully. We took quintessentially Thai dishes like *som tam* and replaced the shaved green papaya with shaved seasonal root vegetables with sweet and earthy tones – carrots, celeriac (celery root) and parsnip – then pounded these into a dressing flavoured with spicy horseradish, sour sea buckthorn berries and sweet local honey. Astonishingly, the taste was deeply rooted in familiar British flavours but the tone was different – it tasted Thai, but with a different expression. This was a light-bulb moment, and is one of the key events that defines the style of food I cook and identify with today, one that represents both sides of my heritage.

After these initial experiences, and years of cooking Thai cuisine in the UK, I have come to believe that Thai food is not solely defined by its ingredients, but instead requires the considerate balancing act of the complex flavours synonymous with the cuisine – salty, sweet, spicy and sour – and these flavours can all be found in the natural British larder. Now when I cook, I use this food philosophy to breathe life into traditional Thai recipes that are beginning to be lost to the country's fast modernisation. Complex, almost tedious recipes that were once passed down from elders in Thai families are now in danger of being lost forever as Thailand's younger generations' lust for convenience meals grows. I believe these traditional recipes demand a voice in the modern food scene, and it would be a travesty for these ancient dishes to be lost forever. My mission is to re-imagine recipes using the finest ingredients from the best local farmers, while always respecting my domestic British surroundings. It's not always easy to achieve, but has become a deeply rooted passion that I feel in my core when cooking. My Thai and British heritage are each represented equally in my cooking. Neither is more or less important; instead, it is a finely tuned balancing act that allows a dish to sing with flavours recognisable from both Western and Asian cultures. The term 'Anglo-Thai' has come to epitomise this ethos and these values, and speaks honestly about my cooking style. It is who I am and what I love to create on a plate. At my restaurant – AngloThai – we use these beliefs to connect guests with our roots in Thailand and Britain through the food and wine we serve, bringing people together in an immersive and experiential journey. With this cookbook, I will look to build on this connection, bringing you along for the journey with me.

I hope this book helps you to approach Thai cooking with a different mindset, giving you the confidence to try cooking new recipes with unconventional ingredients and flavours. Don't be afraid to make mistakes; in fact, I encourage you to make them, learn from them and ultimately grow from them. I know I've made my fair share of errors on my journey with Thai cuisine, and I'd argue I'm all the better for it. Cooking should be fun and it's something that can give you happiness on so many levels. Be enthusiastic, use your curiosity and intuition, but above all, if you remember one thing from this introduction, it's that Thai food doesn't have to be made solely with Thai ingredients. Explore Thai flavours and then think about what local British produce you have available to you that would work as a suitable substitute. It's not always easy, but throughout this book, I hope to help shine a light on some of these ingredients to bring a new style of Thai cooking into your home.

Regions of Thailand

Thailand is located in the centre of mainland Southeast Asia and wholly within the tropics. The kingdom holds all manner of ecosystems, from the cooler forests of the north to the hot and humid coastlines of the southern peninsula. Agriculture was the primary economy up until the latter half of the 20th century, when Western-style modernisation started to influence Thailand, in turn causing people to flock to capital cities such as Bangkok, Chiang Mai and Pattaya. To all intents and purposes, Thailand is broken into four main regions: Central Plains, Northern Thailand (Lanna), Northeastern Thailand (Isaan) and Southern Thailand. They all have different ethnolinguistic backgrounds, different food traditions, varying terroir and different local ingredients, all of which have formed the cuisines of each region.

THE CENTRAL PLAINS

Central Thailand tends to be a melting pot of cultures that draws influences from all over the kingdom, and these influences have always fuelled the imaginations of cooks. This diversity, coupled with the wealth of available ingredients, has resulted in the most complex regional cuisine of Thailand. The Central Plains are also home to the famous floating river market, which lies to the west of the world-renowned capital Bangkok. Many great rivers converge in this delta, making it a fertile plain for rice-growing, and with most land being dedicated to rice production, there is little access to wild and foraged ingredients. Instead, cultivated vegetables are grown using the wealth of rivers and lakes, including spinach, watercress and morning glory. Many other vegetables, including wing beans, snake beans, aubergines (eggplants) and bamboo shoots, are also popular, and these are added to curries and stir-fries or integrated into simple salads with proteins, fresh herbs and dressings made from chillies, lime juice, sugar and fish sauce. Farmed animals, such as chickens, pork and duck, make up a large portion of the central resident's diet. However, rivers and lakes are teeming with life, so river shrimp, freshwater fish, molluscs and shellfish are also extremely popular.

Central Plains dishes are typically more rounded and refined than those found regionally, aided by the prevalent use of coconut cream and sugar. Chinese influence is apparent in wok dishes, the most famous being *pad thai*: flat rice noodles stir-fried with tofu, dried shrimp and bean sprouts in a sweet, tart sauce. Chinese influence also shows up in street foods like fried chive cakes (*kanom gui chai tod*), five-spice braised pork (*mu parlow*) and *pad grapao*, in which protein and vegetables are stir-fried with pungent chillies, garlic and holy basil leaf (*bai grapao*).

The widest variety of curries are eaten in the Central Plains, and many internationally recognised curries, including red curry (*gaeng phet*) and green curry (*gaeng keow wan*), originate in this region. Curries or *gaeng* are usually simmered in meat stocks and coconut milk, or dry-fried, like the incredibly delicious *pad prik king* – a rich, dry red curry of pork and smoked fish. These curries are generally not as fiery as those typical of Southern or Northeastern Thailand, and are instead aromatically scented with lemongrass, galangal, makrut lime and fresh basil. They are predominantly hot and salty, warmed by fragrant chilli peppers, and salted with fish sauce (*nahm pla*) and shrimp paste (*gapi*).

World-renowned soups, such as hot and sour prawn soup (*tom yum goong*) and coconut milk, galangal and chicken soup (*tom kha gai*), also originate in this region, but often taste sweeter compared to those of other regions, as people residing in the Central Plains favour heat and sweetness on the palate above the sourness and fermented pungency found throughout the rest of the kingdom.

Royal Thai cuisine, created during the days of the ancient Ayutthaya court, still influences modern cuisine in Bangkok and its surrounding areas. These are dishes made with expensive ingredients, meticulous spicing and ornate decoration and presentation. Traditionally only made within the royal palace kitchens, these recipes were historically reserved exclusively for the royal family. Now, a younger generation of Thai chefs are unearthing these ancient recipes, giving modern Thai people the chance to taste these refined dishes from the past. Example recipes include the strikingly violet *chor muang*, a Rama II-era steamed rice dumpling stuffed with a sweetened chicken or pork and peanut mixture; sweet and sour crispy rice noodles (*mee krob*); steamed pumpkin stuffed with coconut custard (*sangkaya fak tong*); and beef soup with fermented shrimp paste (*gaeng ranjuan*). While chilli paste relish (*nam prik*) and chilli paste relish simmered in fresh coconut cream (*lon*) are a main staple of every Thai mealtime, when eaten as part of a Royal Thai meal, the accompanying vegetables must always be seeded, peeled and carved or manipulated into attractive shapes. The same goes for fresh fruits, with stones (pits) removed and skins peeled in a special manner called *pak riew*.

Many believe the quintessential Royal Thai dish is *khao chae*, roughly translated as 'soaked rice' and now widely known as 'summertime rice', which is prepared during the hottest season between March and April. This cold rice porridge dish was adapted from the Mon people and introduced during the reign of King Rama IV, who had Mon ancestral roots. The dish traditionally comprises four parts – rice smoked in scented candles used in cooking (*khao ob tien*), jasmine-scented water, ice cubes and side dishes. The latter can vary depending on the cook preparing the dish, but they typically include deep-fried balls made from shrimp paste, grilled snakehead fish, lemongrass and wild ginger (*look gapi*); shredded sweetened pork threads (*mu foi*); fried stuffed shallots with ground catfish (*hom sod sai pla tod*); bell pepper with herbed stuffing wrapped in egg 'lace' (*prik yoak*); melon with ground fish floss and shallot (*tang mo pla haeng*); and intricately carved fresh vegetables and fruits, which are offset against these other sweet dishes. Still prized by Thais today, *khao chae* can be found on menus all over the region, from the most high-end hotel restaurants to humble street-food market stalls. Truly authentic versions of the chilled rice soup require the rice grains to be painstakingly 'polished' in several changes of clean water to avoid clouding of the final porridge.

NORTHERN THAILAND

Northern Thailand is mountainous and more temperate than the rest of the country, with slightly cooler weather experienced all year round. The land is mostly jungle-covered valleys and mountains, with the highest peaks of the country found here. Historically, this area is the home of the Lanna, whose former capital was Chiang Mai, and the north's proximity to China and Myanmar (formerly Burma) has made it a trading centre and cultural crossroads. People like the Tai, Burmese and Chinese, along with the many hill tribes, including the Akkha, Hmong, Yao, Lisu and Tai Yai, have all brought their own foods and cooking styles to the region. Due to the fertile forests and jungle soils, there is an abundance of wild mushrooms, forest vegetables and fruits, and wildlife, all of which feature in this less well-known regional cuisine. The food of the Lanna is characterised by this abundance of flavours and influences, with many typical foods tracing their origins to a number of different cuisines. Thanks to its

inaccessible mountainous terrain, the north's historical isolation has allowed its cuisine to develop uniquely from that of Bangkok and the rest of Thailand.

Favourable agricultural conditions and abundant food has resulted in Northern dishes being milder and less spicy than those of other regions, as it wasn't necessary to encourage diners to eat more rice adorned with fiery chilli pastes, and therefore less meat or vegetables. The predominant flavours in Northern food are hot and salty, with the heat coming from chillies, ginger, galangal and fresh or dried black pepper and long pepper (*dee plee*). The salty taste is traditionally derived from a number of assertive seasoning pastes made from dried fermented soybean discs (*tua nao*), fermented river fish (*pla raa*) and salted rice paddy crabs (*nahm bpu*). Taste profiles of dishes veer towards umami and meaty, but rarely sweet, with liberal use of indigenous forest herbs, not only giving them an aromatic freshness, but also a bitterness and astringency. These are prized flavours among northern people and the local tribes that live on the land.

Prickly ash or *makhwaen* is an indigenous dried spice and a relative of Sichuan peppercorns. The spice can be found in dishes throughout the region and gives the food a distinct peppery-citrus flavour. *Makhwaen* and other dried spices like long pepper (*dee plee*) and *mahlep* (an aromatic spice with a marzipan flavour made from cherry seeds) form the backbone of a spice mix called *prik laab*. This is used to give a deep complexity to hand-chopped meat flavoured with dried spices and blood (*laab mueng*), which is this region's version of the famous *laab* dish also found in Northeastern Thailand (Isaan). Another notable dish from the region is *naem*, where a mixture of chopped pork, pig's skin and garlic is fermented with cooked rice in banana leaf parcels – a truly unique item with a sour-salty-savoury flavour profile seldom found in other cuisines. Other dishes include pork and sour tomato relish (*nahm prik ong*), red curry herbal pork sausage (*sai ua*), grilled chilli relish (*nahm prik num*) and braised pork belly curry with pickled garlic and ginger (*gaeng hung lae*), the latter of these dishes using dried spices from neighbouring Myanmar.

The raising of pigs has historically been part of Northern Thai life, resulting in pork being the protein of choice. Every part of the animal is prized in a multitude of different cooking methods, from gently smoked and grilled pork neck (*mu yang*), to crispy fried ears (*hu mu tort*) and intestine (*dteuu huaan tort*), as well as pork rinds (*kap mu*) and slow-braised shoulder cuts and pork belly. Thai people are incredibly resourceful when it comes to their cooking and eating habits. Whole-carcass eating is celebrated and waste is never an issue. Due to the number of pigs reared in the area, there has traditionally been an abundance of pork fat available for rich, oily dishes and for deep-frying. In addition, forests full of wood have provided plenty of fuel for slow-cooking methods like roasting and braising, as well as for grilling, frying and boiling. Curries and soups in the north tend to be simply prepared and boiled for long periods, yielding some of the most unctuous and delicious braised dishes in the country. On the other hand, dishes influenced by Chinese cuisine are subject to rapid, very hot stir-frying in the wok. Freshwater fish, such as catfish and eels, are common, as are game meats, such as wild boar, deer, rats and frogs. Small, sour cherry tomatoes, young tamarind leaves, green mangoes and bamboo shoots are typical vegetables. Jackfruit is an important ingredient, eaten both ripe and sweet as a fruit, and young and starchy as a savoury vegetable. Sticky rice is a staple grain as in the neighbouring Isaan region, but steamed jasmine rice and brown rice are also widely eaten.

A favourite dish with locals and foreigners alike is Chiang Mai's famous curried noodle soup (*khao soi*), a fragrant bowl of aromatic coconut curry soup flavoured with dried spices and served over soft egg noodles, usually with tender braised beef or chicken. Bowls are topped with crispy fried egg noodles, pickled mustard greens and fresh Thai shallots drizzled with a deep crimson chilli oil. The dish may have originated with the Burmese Shan or the Chinese Muslim Yunnan, and the name *khao soi* illustrates its mix of possible sources, literally meaning 'enter the lane'. Perhaps this refers to the location of the stands where this dish was introduced on tiny *soi* (side streets). There is a Burmese noodle dish with a similar name and composition, and as parts of the north were under Burmese control for hundreds of years, it is understandable that these dishes would share similarities. There are many vendors famous for this dish in and around Chiang Mai, and thousands of bowlfuls are consumed each day as a result of its popularity.

NORTHEASTERN THAILAND

Northeastern Thailand is commonly referred to as Isaan and is a wide plateau, with the Mekong River forming the border with Laos to the north and Cambodia to the south. The climate is extreme, swinging between a hot, dry season and an extremely wet season, causing yearly droughts and floods. Rice does not grow consistently here, and nor do most other crops, making it Thailand's poorest region economically, both historically and today. Most of the rivers that cross the Isaan plateau flow into the Mekong rather than towards Central Thailand. As this complicates water travel into Central Thailand, the Isaan region shares much culturally, linguistically and culinarily with its neighbouring countries, with many Lao and Khmer-speaking people residing in Isaan today.

The food of Isaan tends to be very spicy due to the use of chillies, and has a distinctive salty, pungent flavour from the use of *nahm pla raa*, a thick almost rustic-style of fish sauce made from fermented river fish. There are two dishes held in the highest esteem among the people of Isaan, pounded green papaya salad (*som tam*) and hand-chopped meat (*laab*), with both available in many variations and styles. There are actually two main types of *som tam*: Thai-style, which calls for the addition of dried shrimp, roasted peanuts, tomatoes and fish sauce; and Lao-style, which is pounded with fermented black crab (*nahm bpu*) and *nahm pla raa*. As might be expected, both contain fierce amounts of fresh and/or dried chillies. Isaan-style *laab* dishes, like those of Laos, are often made of raw meat, finely hand chopped using specialist *laab* knives and 'cooked' ceviche-style in an acidic sauce. Many other Isaan dishes are similarly acidic, using citrus and sour fruits such as tamarind and hog plums. Coconut cream and sugar rarely feature in the region's cuisine.

As this is the poorest region of Thailand, the intense flavours of Isaan dishes are a way of managing an insecure food supply – very hot, flavourful dishes encourage diners to diffuse and season large quantities of filling sticky rice during mealtimes (this is the favoured starch, rather than the jasmine rice eaten throughout the rest of Thailand). Cooking methods could be described as rustic and somewhat crude, with cooks favouring simple techniques, such as grilling and boiling. A large range of cured, pickled and raw dishes take centre stage, due to the lack of trees available for wood fuel. Dishes are relatively simple, employing a smaller range of spices and seasonings compared with other regions of Thailand.

Other famous dishes include grilled chicken (*gai yang*) and grilled pork neck (*kor mu yang*) served with fermented fish dipping sauce spiked with chillies and tamarind (*nahm jim jaew*), as well as hot and sour herbal soup (*tom sap*), charred meat dressed with herbs, dried chillies and toasted rice powder (*nahm tok*), and rice fermented pork sausage (*sai krok*), this region's version of the north's *naem*. Many fresh herbs and raw vegetables are used in abundance to counterbalance the intense heat and pungency of Isaan food. Rather surprisingly, dill, known throughout the region as Isaan coriander (cilantro), is used as commonly as regular coriander is in central Thailand. Isaan people enjoy eating water buffalo in dishes like *laap* and *nahm tok* where the fiery nature of the supporting ingredients masks the strong flavour of the buffalo meat. Similarly, jungle creatures such as lizards and frogs also make their way on to Isaan menus, as do ingredients as unlikely as red ant eggs, which are prized for their sour and creamy taste. Despite this rustic and simple approach, the dishes found in Isaan are irresistibly satisfying in their intensely gobsmacking and punchy flavours, and the region's cuisine has spread widely throughout the Kingdom of Thailand and overseas with its travelling people.

SOUTHERN THAILAND

Southern Thailand refers to the area south of Bangkok, continuing down into the *Kra Isthmus* (Thai Canal or Kra Canal), the narrowest part of the Malay Peninsula, which is bordered on the west by Myanmar, and widens as it reaches the Malaysian borders. In contrast to the other areas of the kingdom, rice is not the major crop. Instead, agriculture is focused around coconuts and bananas, while the majority of fresh fish and seafood that makes its way on to restaurant menus is caught directly in the south. The south has an abundance of coconut palms, which grow along the shores of the Gulf Sea, and this is reflected in the liberal use of coconut milk and cream in southern dishes. Food in the south is renowned for being complex and strong in taste – very hot, salty and sour. Spicy curries are eaten every day, especially sour curries, and generally southerners eat more fish and seafood than meat, because they reside so close to the sea.

Southern food is the hottest in Thailand, often seasoned with tiny fresh bird's eye chillies (*prik kii nuu suan*) and commonly tastes salty and, of course, incredibly sour. Southern curries are coloured red, yellow and orange, thanks to the liberal use of red chillies and turmeric root. The latter is also used to diffuse unwanted strong seafood odours and flavours, with cooks liberally rubbing turmeric into the flesh of fish and other seafood prior to cooking. Examples include sour orange curry flavoured with tamarind (*gaeng som*) and dry turmeric curry of minced (ground) pork, lemongrass, makrut lime leaf and chillies (*kua kling mu*). Coconut oil and milk are often boiled with fruits, such as pineapple, papaya and tamarind, to balance their richness, with dishes including rich coconut cream and turmeric curry (*gaeng gati*) and thin yellow curry with pineapple (*gaeng lueng*). However, one of the region's most famous dishes goes completely against the grain of these other Southern curries. *Gaeng tai pla* is a notoriously pungent, spicy and salty eating experience. It's made with fermented fish innards, and is a firm favourite among locals for breakfast, lunch and dinner.

When central-style curries, such as green and red, are prepared in the south, they are usually hotter, and a larger quantity of shrimp paste (*gapi*) is added to intensify their flavours. The thicker curries made by Thai Muslims often use ghee or yoghurt in place of coconut, while dried spices, like white cardamom, cassia bark and nutmeg, are added to curry pastes, giving extra complexity and depth to these dishes compared to those of other Thai regions. The prevalent Muslim community has a different culinary preference to the Thai community. Beef, mutton and goat feature in richer curries with dried spices, such as Muslim dry-spiced coconut curry (*gaeng mussaman*), while a rich coconut curry sauce is used to marinate chicken and pork before being slowly barbecued (grilled) over charcoal (*gaeng gola*). A similar dish is the world-renowned *satay* (peanut coconut sauce), where slivers of chicken or beef are threaded on to sticks and again barbecued (grilled) over charcoal, served with a spicy peanut sauce and a relish of pickled cucumber, shallot and chillies (*ajut*). *Khao yam* is a crunchy breakfast 'rice salad' of steamed jasmine rice, usually coloured blue with pea flowers and served with roasted coconut, roasted chilli powder (*prik bon*), finely shredded makrut lime leaves, wild pepper leaf (*bai champoo*), lemongrass, dried shrimp powder and a variety of local vegetables and fruits, intended to bring contrasting flavours and textures. It is dressed with a spicy-sour-sweet sauce that uses citrus, chilli and fermented ocean fish sauce (*nahm budu*), a truly unique flavour to Southern Thailand.

Freshly caught seafood is used liberally and forms a major part of the southerner's everyday diet due to the huge coastline that hugs the *Kar Isthmus*. Seafood is often barbecued (grilled) and served with a seafood dipping sauce (*nahm jim talay*) made from fresh chillies, garlic, citrus and fish sauce. Alternatively, it is roasted in pots filled with sea salt, like salt-roasted prawns/ shrimp (*gung pao*); boiled in thin stock-based curries, such as sour orange fish curry (*gaeng som pla*); or simply deep-fried, then topped with crispy garlic and turmeric (*pla tort kamin*). Thai Muslims street-food vendors sell deep-fried fish and chicken with bags of sticky rice and sweet chilli sauce or a ladleful of fish sauce laced with fresh chillies (*prik nahm pla*). This style of fried street food is now found on street corners throughout Thailand. Numerous seasonal vegetables are available all year round, along with tropical fruits like mango, pineapple and papaya, which are served both ripe and unripe with a sugar salt mix spiced with chillies (*prik gleua*).

Fermented shrimp paste (*gapi*) is fundamental in southern cooking. Perhaps the most popular dish originating in the south is shrimp paste relish (*nahm prik gapi*), something of an ancient national dish for the Kingdom of Thailand. It represents a side of Thai cuisine seldom known outside its homeland. This relish is distinctly salty and pungent from *gapi*, spicy from the fistfuls of fresh *prik kii nu suan* (literal translation 'rat dropping chillies') and sour from freshly squeezed lime juice. When it comes to eating *nahm prik gapi*, a little goes a long way, and that's exactly why this dish has become a main staple of Thai cuisine. Eaten with plenty of freshly steamed jasmine rice and an array of boiled or raw vegetables, the relish is more of a seasoning that bridges the meal and provides flavour to an otherwise bland set of ingredients, essential when making food stretch. It's also made from ingredients accessible to any Thai household, regardless of status and wealth.

The British Isles

The British Isles is a rich and fertile collection of islands in the North Sea, made up of Great Britain (England, Scotland and Wales), Ireland (Republic of Ireland and Northern Ireland), the Isle of Man and the Channel Islands, together offering an incredibly diverse range of edible produce. Between them, the islands boast nearly 20,000 miles of coastline, providing a bounty of wild seafood, shellfish and coastal plant life. Scotland's clear, cold waters are ideal conditions for producing some of the best langoustines and lobsters in the world, as well as shellfish such as scallops, razor clams and mussels. These waters not only yield seafood, but are also plentiful with edible seaweeds and coastline herbs, such as sea aster and sea arrowgrass, the latter with a flavour reminiscent of coriander (cilantro). Sea buckthorn, a native orange berry, also grows along the coastline, and has a distinctively sour taste that has notes of mango, passionfruit and tart pineapple. Ireland is home to one of my favourite oyster varieties, an ingredient I use regularly both at home and on my restaurant menus. That's not to say there aren't many other wonderful oyster varieties native to the British Isles; Morecambe Bay in the Lake District, Maldon in Essex, Porthilly in Cornwall and Jersey in the Channel Islands all produce fine oysters. The southwest of England, namely Cornwall and Devon, provide all manner of ocean fish, including mackerel, turbot, lemon sole and skate, as well as crabs, clams and mussels. Only a few inland wild river fish like salmon and trout remain

popular, and native species, such as pike, bream and carp, are rarely eaten.

On the mainland, there is an abundance of arable land capable of being ploughed and used to grow crops, or for raising and nurturing livestock. Farmed animals, such as beef, pork, lamb and chicken, make up the largest proportion of protein eaten in the British Isles. However, game animals, such as roe deer, rabbit and hare, and wild birds, like grouse, mallard, pheasant and partridge, are all eaten when in season. Heritage grains are widely grown on arable land, with wheat, barley and oats making up the majority. These are commonly milled into flours used in bread making. Four main seasons dictate the agriculture of the British Isles; winter, spring, summer and autumn (fall), offering a wide and diverse range of plants, vegetables, fruits and herbs, not only from commercial agriculture but also the wild larder. Hardier brassicas (cabbages, kale and broccoli, to name a few) and root vegetables (carrots, beetroot, celeriac and onions) grow all year round, while salads, peas, beans, courgettes (zucchini) and tomatoes all flourish in the warmer months. The summer also sees delicious berries, which can be foraged from hedgerows, while some of the finest strawberries in the world are grown in Kent in the south of England. Stone (pit) fruits such as plums, damsons, apricots and peaches all grow well, as do our many species of apples and pears. These are not only eaten, but also pressed for cider and perry.

When cooking, I look to move with the

seasons, adapting restaurant menus based on seasonality and sustainability of growth for farmers. You will not find Mediterranean-grown tomatoes featured on my winter menus. Instead, I will wait to champion Isle of Wight-grown heritage tomatoes in their prime summer months. The same logic applies to the use of wonderful Wye Valley asparagus and Kent strawberries. This is not to say the cooler months do not offer incredible produce; it is a time to consider those root vegetables, hardy brassicas and alliums mentioned before. Cooking with the seasons isn't just important for freshness of produce, but is also a responsibility we must all share when it comes to maintaining sustainability. Supporting local farmers and the domestic industry instead of importing unnecessarily is a major contributor to reducing our carbon footprint on the world and is interconnected with fresh, delicious and healthy British Isles produce.

Despite the bounty of produce available in the British Isles, it's impossible to talk about Thai cuisine without mentioning particular indigenous Thai ingredients, such as lemongrass, galangal, coconut, Thai basil and the plethora of other wild and exotic ingredients that Thai cooks have at their disposal. Many of these ingredients only grow and thrive in tropical environments, but it's important to consider the vast array of equally wonderful ingredients grown here in the British Isles. Not only do these domestic ingredients grow with a lower carbon footprint, but they also grow to their full potential due to the hard work of the farmers. Many of these indigenously grown ingredients share the same properties as ingredients found in Thailand. Rhubarb, gooseberries and sea buckthorn are fine examples of seasonal British fruits that have sour acidic profiles similar to citrus fruits and tamarind. Horseradish root and mustard seeds hold the heat and spice level of chillies, local honey has a sweet depth of flavour comparable to palm sugar, and British seafood can be preserved in the style of Roman *garum* to give the properties of umami and salty fish sauce. We will not exclusively use these ingredients in this book, but it is important to understand that the overlap between Western and Asian larders aren't as few as you may at first think. Substitution is all part of the culinary journey and is one of the parameters that I most enjoy exploring in the food I cook today. It goes without saying that my knowledge and experience with ingredient substitution is firmly rooted within my British homeland, but these fundamental principles of adapting ingredients can be applied globally, based on the seasonal produce available wherever you are.

Using This Book

The main aim of this book is to get more people cooking Thai food and to dispel some of the myths that Thai food is overly complicated and too labour intensive for the home kitchen. Yes, it is true that certain Thai dishes require time and a methodical approach, but equally there are so many Thai dishes that are simple to put together and can be made by anyone. If you've ever been to Thailand and eaten at a little ramshackle shop or from a street-corner vendor you will see their cooking set-up is fairly limited, making use of a small charcoal grill or single-burner stove to cook a whole array of dishes. Thai people are extremely resourceful cooks and look to extract the most possible flavour from their dishes by using pungent seasonings and strong-flavoured ingredients, some of which will, of course, be hard to source outside of Thailand. When this is the case I have looked to provide substitute ingredients where possible, but it's worth mentioning that it would be hard to make a curry paste without some core Asian ingredients, such as chillies, lemongrass and galangal. Such ingredients are now widely available in Asian supermarkets (grocery stores) or online (see pages 31–37 for more information on ingredients). In this section, I will touch upon some key advice to help you navigate the recipes in this book and hopefully pass on some of my experience from cooking Thai cuisine over the last years.

TASTING, SEASONING AND BALANCE

It goes without saying that you should taste your food and the ingredients you cook with as you go, not only for Thai recipes but for any cooking you do. Without tasting, how can you know if a dish needs more of a certain seasoning? It would be impossible, and since you have a mouth to taste with, you should use it! When teaching chefs, I can't stress enough how important this is, not only to check for seasoning but to understand the journey the flavours are heading in. Something as simple as a diced onion changes in flavour and character as it sweats in a saucepan with oil and salt; it starts to release its moisture, which intensifies the onion's flavour, becoming sweeter as it caramelises. This is a great example of a single ingredient changing dramatically in flavour as it cooks. Ingredients of the same kind also differ from one to another. One bird's eye chilli might be breathtakingly spicy, while the next might be surprisingly mild. Likewise, one brand of fish or soy sauce may feel saltier than another. It's best to try your ingredients in their raw state so you can understand what each will bring to the party, especially if you aren't familiar with some of the ingredients listed in these recipes. In contrast to Western cuisine, where salt, pepper and vinegar are key seasonings, for Thai cooks there is a whole arson of seasonings available to change the flavour of a dish: salty fish sauce, sweet palm sugar, spicy chillies, sour citrus and funky ferments to name a few. Because of this, I have tried to explain the final seasoning you are looking to achieve in each recipe, but ultimately the final say is yours and yours alone. Taste the food, try to understand what it might be missing to give the dish a balance and roundedness, and adjust with your newly acquired set of seasonings. If you feel like something is too aggressively seasoned, then don't forget most Thai dishes are designed to be eaten with bland rice, so the flavours need to not only season the dish, but also the accompanying starchy rice grains. As you cook more from this book and your confidence grows, so will your ability to know what is missing from a dish and how adding a certain ingredient will affect the final flavour. It will come as no surprise to hear that I wasn't born with a finely tuned palate for tasting and seasoning Thai food. Quite the contrary, in fact, and even today I still encounter new ingredients that surprise my taste buds. Personally, I relish the idea of tasting new flavours and ingredient combinations, and I would encourage you to embrace the journey you are about to embark on with Thai food.

Lime juice

Limes are used widely in Thai cuisine to give sourness and bring brightness to a dish. You might be surprised to hear that the limes we have available to us in Britain are different from those that grow in Southeast Asia. The most common variety of lime available worldwide is the Persian lime, with its thick, waxy skin, seedless interior and sharp citrus flavour. Thai limes have a thinner skin and are generally smaller, with more seeds. The juice of Thai limes is more fragrant and fruitier, with an almost sweet-sour flavour. Because of this, I tend to squeeze the quantity of lime juice I plan to use for a recipe and then doctor the flavour with a squeeze of mandarin or clementine juice. The natural sweetness of these citrus fruits offsets the intense sourness and occasional bitterness of Persian lime juice, giving a juice that is more comparable to that used in Thailand. Tweaking the flavour of your lime juice isn't a necessary step, but I find that most people I have mentioned this juice hack to are blown away by the difference it can bring to the final seasoning of a dish.

Onions vs shallots

I use both onions and shallots throughout the book. Does it actually make a difference if you use one over another in a recipe? Does anyone actually care? Well, you might not, but I'm just going to go into a few differences that will allow you to make up your own mind on the subject. In general, onions are sharper in taste than their sweeter shallot cousins. Of course, onions range in pungency from the very strong white onion to the more versatile and softer yellow onion, right through to the mild red onion. Throughout Thailand, smaller red shallots are commonly used due to their versatile mild and sweet flavour, appearing in everything from robust curry pastes to fragrant salads and perfumed soups. Thai red shallots can be found in Asian supermarkets (grocery stores) but they are relatively expensive and the air miles do them no favours. Instead, I always use a combination of British-grown onions and shallots depending on the dish I'm cooking. I tend to use larger banana shallots for curry pastes, while reaching for smaller red onions for salads. I have listed which type of onion or shallot for each recipe in the book, but ultimately you can use what is available to you.

KNIFE TECHNIQUES

There are plenty of overlaps between Thai and Western knife work, with rustic cooking employing the usual cutting, dicing, slicing and mincing (very finely chopping) techniques that most home cooks are familiar with. Often ingredients are cut into almost crude, bite-size chunks by Thai cooks, favouring irregular pieces that give a contrast of texture in the mouth over the traditional French *brunoise* (small dice) or *julienne* (thin matchsticks). Intensely flavoured ingredients are often finely shredded so that their flavour doesn't dominate a dish. Opposite is a selection of ingredients that are commonly prepared in this fashion. I've given a little additional information on how to prepare each of these ingredients prior to shredding in order to achieve the best results and optimum flavour. A sharp knife is essential for such knife work.

Makrut lime leaves

First, remove the thick seam or rib that holds the two sides of the leaf together. Once this is done, fold the leaf in half lengthways along the seam and stack a few similar-sized leaves on top of each other; I would start with about three leaves until you have mastered this technique. Fold the stack in half, this time across the width of the leaves, then using your knife, trim the torn edge where the seam once was to create a single straight side. Now take your time as you cut the stack of leaves as thinly as possible. Once you get good at this, you will produce wispy, thin pieces of lime leaf that can be used to garnish dishes or sprinkle through salads. This technique only works with fresh or frozen makrut lime leaves and not with dried leaves; I don't recommend bothering with dried at all, as their flavour is dull and lifeless.

Fresh long chillies

Slice the top and stalk off the chilli then split it lengthways. Remove the seeds and membrane then gently flatten the chilli against your cutting board. Carefully run your knife along the inside of the chilli to cut away some of the flesh, leaving about 1 mm ($1/_{32}$ in) of the skin and flesh – this will take some practice. Cut the chilli into 3 cm (1¼ in) pieces, then slice these lengthways into 1 mm ($1/_{32}$ in) thin strands. These chilli strands can now be used in salads, or tumbled with other toppings for *miang* (one-bite snacks) when cooking appetisers for a dinner.

Lemongrass

Prepare the lemongrass by cutting the bottom root from the stalk to reveal the pale heart; depending on the lemongrass this will require cutting around 3 cm (1¼ in) from the stalk. Remove the fibrous outer husk layers (around 2–3 layers) to leave the tender, pale yellow lemongrass heart. Start slicing from the thicker root end, cutting as thinly as possible, but stop once you feel resistance as you hit the tougher green top. After some practice, you will be able to slice the lemongrass into wafer-thin 1 mm ($1/_{32}$ in) slices that can be used in salads and as garnish to dishes. As an approximation, one large fresh lemongrass stalk should yield around 1 heaped tablespoon of sliced lemongrass. Keep hold of any scraps, as they are packed full of flavour and can be used to infuse stocks, braises and brines.

HOME PANTRY

When you flick through the recipes in this book, you might feel daunted by the many new ingredients that are required to cook some of the dishes. I will confess, it will be hard to cook these recipes without investing in some new items, but many of the dried or preserved ingredients, such as palm sugar, seasoning sauces, shrimp paste and dried chillies, will last almost indefinitely in your cupboard or refrigerator. Many fresh ingredients can also be prepared and stored in your freezer by peeling, cleaning and portioning before freezing for months (more on this and storecupboard ingredients on pages 31–37). It's also true to say that a Thai cook relies on a different pantry of items compared to a Western cook. Toasted chilli powder (*prik bon*), tamarind water (*nahm makham piak*) and fried shallots (*hom jiaw*) aren't commonly found items in Western supermarkets (grocery stores) so you may have to make these from scratch. That being said, they will last well and can be made in large batches, so your larder is stocked for a few months without having to repeat the process. Over time, you will build up a pantry that boasts a variety of items that will easily enable you to make most dishes from this book.

MEASUREMENTS

Measurements are given in teaspoons and tablespoons as well as metric weights or volumes, depending on whether the ingredient is solid or liquid. In the restaurant we weigh everything, including liquids, as this gives the most accurate measurement. Decent compact digital scales cost very little, so my suggestion would be to treat yourself and get used to weighing your ingredients. That way, you can be sure of accuracy the first time you cook these recipes, ultimately giving you the best chance of successfully making the dishes as I have intended. As you become more familiar with cooking Thai cuisine, your experience and confidence will grow, making this requirement to meticulously weigh every ingredient less important. Instead you will be able to rely more on your intuition and senses to feel out the recipe.

ASSEMBLING A THAI MEAL

Even after you have mastered cooking the recipes in this book, there are a few points to consider when it comes to putting a Thai meal together. Unlike in Western culture, the emphasis in Thailand is on a selection of dishes that provide contrasting flavours and textures, but come together as a balanced, coherent meal. At the heart of almost every meal is steamed rice or sometimes noodles, served with dishes that take the palate from savoury to sweet, tart to salty and spicy to mild. Dancing between these flavours gives the diner a truly memorable eating experience and overall balance when all the dishes of the meal are eaten as a whole. The concept of a shared family mealtime should be familiar enough for people who grew up eating traditional Sunday roasts with a centrepiece roasted joint, starchy potatoes, savoury gravy and accompanying fresh vegetables. Essentially, everyone builds their own plate from the communal dishes at the centre of the table. Where possible, I have offered suggestions of dishes that work well together, but as a general rule of thumb, if you are cooking for a group, then aim to have a curry, salad, relish, soup, stir-fry and, of course, rice, with a contrast of flavours and textures across the dishes. For instance, if I was serving a spicy curry such as venison jungle curry (*gaeng ba kwang*), then a mild, soothing soup like Coconut and Galangal Soup of Wild Mushrooms (*dtom kha hed ba*) (page 98) would complement this nicely, as would a tart and refreshing salad, such as Green Apple and Crispy Dried Anchovy Salad (*yum aepbpeern*) (page 51). It is also worth noting that Thai people favour a spoon and fork rather than the common knife-and-fork combination we adopt in the Western world. This is because Thai dishes are purposely prepared so that everything is bite-size and does not require any further cutting. The spoon is also handy when it comes to scooping up the many saucy and soupy dishes, as well as the rice grains. Traditionally, silverware was forgone in favour of eating with hands, a practice that still lives on in regions where sticky rice is king (Northern and Northeastern Thailand). There, people shape a clump of sticky rice into an edible spoon shape before scooping and dipping at the accompanying dishes. I don't suggest you need to practise this way of eating, but it's nice to know that you wouldn't be out of place in parts of Isaan by eating with your hands.

Ingredients

It is worth noting that one of the most important traits in Thai cooking is resourcefulness: adopting the mindset that something delicious can normally be created using the ingredients that are available and to hand. My food philosophy dictates that if you don't have a certain Asian ingredient available to you, then you should think about what can be used as a substitute rather than forgo a recipe completely. In some circumstances, the ingredient might be true to the traditional recipe, but actually omitting it may cause little to no difference. It's always worth considering these facts, and it will enable you to become a more intuitive cook. That being said, there are a number of Asian ingredients that I can't live without because they hold specific flavour profiles that would be hard to replicate. The good news is that the majority of these items are storecupboard ingredients that last almost indefinitely, are relatively cheap to buy and these days can be found in an Asian supermarket (grocery store), where they will be cheaper and of better quality than in a regular supermarket. You could even consider buying online – thai-food-online.co.uk is a great online shop. You don't necessarily need to buy everything at once: perhaps choose some staples that pop up across multiple recipes, such as fish sauce, shrimp paste, palm sugar and dried chillies, then look to grow your storecupboard from there. Once you have the bulk of these ingredients at home, you will be equipped to cook any number of Asian recipes, not just the Thai dishes in this cookbook.

STORECUPBOARD

These are the essentials that I have in the cupboard or refrigerator at all times to cook a selection of Thai dishes at home. I have stated which brands I buy and it's probably no surprise to hear I buy products made in Thailand, where 'Product of Thailand' is stipulated somewhere on the packaging. If you can't source a specific Thai brand, then look out for Southeast Asian or Chinese brands that make the same product.

Fish sauce ● *nahm pla*
This sauce is made by salting and fermenting anchovies for many years, producing an amber liquor that is quintessential to Thai cuisine. There are countless commercial brands available, with Squid and Tiparos being two of the most popular from Thailand. If I'm looking for a less sharp saltiness, I reach for Megachef brand: although slightly more expensive than rival brands, it has a higher anchovy ratio and no nasty added extras.

Light soy sauce ● *nahm see uu khao*
A main staple for many Thai dishes that have a Chinese influence, this is a thinner, saltier seasoning sauce than black soy sauce. The two are not a like-for-like substitute. Light soy sauce can be used for cooking as well as seasoning, dressings and dipping sauces. I use Healthy Boy brand and Megachef, the latter of which is, rather usefully, gluten-free.

Black soy sauce • *nahm see uu dam*

Also known as dark soy sauce and much thicker than light soy sauce, black soy sauce has a sweeter caramel flavour from the addition of molasses. Its main purpose is to give depth of flavour and colour to dishes during cooking. I favour Healthy Boy brand, but in some circumstances the Indonesian sweet soy (*ketjap manis*) is used in recipes; in those instances, look for Lucullus brand.

Seasoning sauce • *nahm proong ros*

This is the secret ingredient in many Thai recipes, particularly stir-fries. Although not commonly known in the Western world, this sauce has been used in Thailand for centuries. Like soy sauce, it's made from fermented soybeans, but it has a more rounded flavour from the addition of sugar and 'flavour enhancers' (not MSG) to give deeper umami that balances the saltiness. The main brand used throughout Thailand is Golden Mountain, or affectionately known as 'green cap' due to the colour of the bottle top.

Oyster sauce • *nahm man hoi*

An essential when you want to give an almost smoky umami depth to dishes, this dark, viscous sauce has a distinctive briny-salty-sweet flavour that is derived from reduced and caramelised oyster extract. Once opened, it's best to keep it in the refrigerator for maximum freshness, where it will happily keep indefinitely. My go-to brands are Maekrua and Megachef.

Yellow soybean sauce • *nahm dtow jiaw*

As the name suggests, this sauce is made from yellow soybeans that are fermented with rice mould (or *koji*) into a salty-sweet-umami sauce that has many applications in Thai cookery, from the famous chicken rice (*khao man gai*) to stir-fried water spinach (*pak bung fai dang*). I liken the flavour to Japanese miso or Korean *doenjang*, which I often cook with to add a salty umami depth. Healthy Boy yellow soybean sauce is the brand to buy.

Palm sugar • *nahm dtaan bpeuk*

A golden-brown sugar that's derived from the sap of palm trees and boiled in vats to create a thick paste, this is used to season all manner of dishes. Slightly confusingly, coconut sugar is made from the buds of coconut tree flowers. Keep in mind that the names palm and coconut sugar are often used interchangeably, and for all intents and purposes can qualify for the same role. I prefer the brighter sweetness of palm sugar, but if you can only find coconut sugar, it won't prove detrimental to your cooking. I buy Thai brands Maesri or Aroy-D, which are 100 per cent palm sugar.

Tamarind • *makhaam*

A brown-skinned pod containing fibrous fruit that is both sweet and sour. Tamarind pulp is commonly available, and is made by ripening the flesh and drying it in the sun until it's a deep cocoa colour. The pulp simply needs rehydrating with warm water before straining to remove fibres and seeds. The resulting water has a lovely tartness and is used in salads, soups, curries and sweets (candies). Ready-made tamarind concentrate can be bought commercially; it lacks some of the sourness of freshly made, but for convenience, it's fine to use. Cock Brand is reliable for both tamarind pulp and concentrate.

Shrimp paste • *gapi*

The very soul of Thai cuisine, you either love it or hate it. Fortunately, I side with my Thai heritage and love the stuff. It is made by grinding tiny shrimp with salt and leaving them to ferment for up to a year or more. *Gapi* is very powerful stuff and a little goes a long way. It also lasts indefinitely in the refrigerator. There are a few Thai brands to look out for: Nang Fah (red tub), Pantai (pink tub) and Maepranom (purple tub).

Dried shrimp • *goong haeng*

Essentially small shrimp that have been salted and air-dried in the sun. You can buy whatever size you like, but I find the medium size, about 15 mm ($^2/_3$ in), are the most universal and versatile. It's worth soaking them in warm water to clean and rehydrate the shrimp before using.

Coconut cream and coconut milk • *hua gati/hang gati*

Commonly found in most supermarkets (grocery stores) in can or box packaging, but not to be confused with the thin opaque coconut water. Always try to buy pure, unsweetened varieties. By that, I mean with no emulsifiers and funny business added – just coconut and water. There are some decent Thai brands on the market, including Chaokoh, Mae Ploy and Aroy-D, all of which have a high percentage of coconut to water. The taste of freshly made coconut cream is incomparable in its complexity and deliciousness, but for convenience, shop-bought is absolutely fine, and I often use it at home. A note on how to make fresh coconut cream later (pages 208–209) for those intrepid cooks.

Dried chillies • *prik haeng*
There are two categories of dried chillies used in Thai cooking. The first are small, hot bird's eye chillies, which are used to make *prik bon* (toasted chilli powder) and form the backbone of the intensely fierce food of Southern Thailand. The second are the larger, fleshy red chillies that have a milder heat and form the basis of red curries. If you're having trouble finding Thai dried chillies, then Mexican dried chillies hold similar attributes and can be bought online (coolchile.co.uk). When Thai chillies aren't available, I use *chilli de arbol* and *guajillo* in place of bird's eye and long red chillies respectively.

Rice • *khao*
The backbone of almost every meal in Thailand. Rarely is there not a bowl of steamed jasmine rice (*khao hom mali*) or glutinous sticky rice (*khao niaw*) as the centrepiece of the table, with all accompanying dishes as supporting acts. If you have eaten Thai food before, you are probably aware that rice is the perfect sponge for soaking up the intensely rich and pungent flavours, ultimately providing balance to the meal. I recommend buying long-grain jasmine rice, known as *khao hom mali* in Thailand, which translates as 'fragrant jasmine rice'. When it comes to sticky rice, look again for rice grown in Thailand, which is sometimes labelled glutinous rice.

Curry paste • *khreuang gaeng*
I would always recommend taking the time to make your own curry paste, as the differences between freshly made and shop-bought pastes are huge. Saying this, when time is scarce or fresh Thai ingredients are unavailable, then having a good-quality shop-bought paste in the refrigerator never hurt anyone. You can easily adapt a shop-bought paste by adding more chillies, aromatics or dried spices to suit other recipes. For those starting out and not wanting to invest in all the ingredients required to make a curry paste from scratch, then a shop-bought paste can be a great option, allowing for convenience and helping build confidence before you move on to the next level of cooking Thai food. Nittaya or Mae Ploy are both good commercial curry paste brands, but be aware they have a high salt content in order to preserve the paste for longer, so be sure to adjust your seasoning accordingly.

DRIED SPICES
Over my years of cooking at home, I have built up quite a collection of dried spices. I'm not an advocate for keeping dried spices indefinitely, but generally speaking, if you find yourself cooking fairly regularly from this book, then you will almost inadvertently put together a small collection of dried spices that will probably be depleted before losing their fragrance or going out of date. There are specific recipes that call for dried spices, such as Burmese Pork Belly Curry (*gaeng hung lae*) (page 144) and Northern Thai chopped meat (*laab muang*), but you will find dried spices are most commonly used across different curry pastes to add depth and intensity against the fresh ingredients. You don't need to buy all (or any) of the dried spices listed below, but I've provided an explanation of a few of the more interesting Thai-specific dried spices I keep at home.

White cardamom • *luk grawan*
Traditionally, this was an uncommon spice in the Thai repertoire, but it is now found in dishes of Muslim origin. Not to be mistaken with the green and black cardamom used in Indian cookery, this is a small white pod that houses black seeds. The whole pod is dry-toasted before being added to curries and braises, or being cracked open to extract the seeds, which are used in curry pastes.

Prickly ash • *makhwaen*
An uncommon spice that is indigenous to Northern Thailand and is indispensable in the Northern Thai spice blend (*prik laab*), which forms the backbone of this region's cuisine. *Makhwaen* is a relative of Sichuan peppercorns

and imparts a distinct peppery-citrus flavour. Sichuan peppercorns can be used as a substitute when *makhwaen* is called for.

Cassia bark • *op choey*
A relative of cinnamon, but with a much thicker, bark-like quill that is richer in flavour, cassia bark can be toasted and added to braises, releasing its sweet taste. Cinnamon is a fine substitute if you can't source cassia.

Peppercorns • *prik thai*
White peppercorns are the most widely used in Thailand for seasoning, and provided heat to dishes before the Portuguese brought the chilli pepper to Thailand in around 1511. A 'holy trinity' paste of white peppercorns, coriander (cilantro) root and garlic (sometimes with the addition of a fourth ingredient, ginger) is one of the oldest seasoning pastes, and is still frequently used today. Thai cooks also enjoy using fresh green peppercorns, which can be eaten whole and give an enjoyably hot and bright peppery flavour.

Coriander seeds • *luuk pak chii*
Thai coriander seeds are darker, smaller and more intense in flavour than regular coriander seeds, but I wouldn't worry about hunting down specific Thai ones; regular will do.

Dried orange peel • *piw som haeng*
This is used in braises and soups to give a lovely sweet background flavour. I make my own by drying mandarin and clementine peels in a low oven (55°C/130°F/lowest possible gas) or dehydrator until bone dry, then storing in an airtight container.

Curry powder • *pong karii*
Thai cooks favour a relatively mild, turmeric -coloured curry powder for dishes such as curried crab (*bpu pad pong karii*) and Muslim spiced oxtail soup (*sup hang wua*). A shop-bought mild Indian or madras curry powder is a fine substitution when required.

Long pepper • *dee plee*
A cylindrical, long and thin dark spice that has an almost citrussy, peppery flavour, this a key ingredient in the Northern Thai spice blend *prik laab*. There is no substitution.

FRESH INGREDIENTS: AROMATICS AND HERBS

I tend to stray away from buying too many fresh ingredients that carry lots of air miles from overseas, for all the obvious reasons. That being said, it's difficult to cook Thai food without a certain number of fresh ingredients that bring Thai soul to your dishes. Here's a list of ingredients I keep in the refrigerator to achieve a great range of Thai cooking at home. In many situations, these fresh ingredients can be prepared and portioned for storage in the freezer, so you don't need to rely on going to the Asian supermarket (grocery store) as frequently.

Makrut lime and makrut lime leaf • *luk makrut/bai makrut*
The fruit is highly prized for its knobbly zest, which adds vibrant citrus notes to curry pastes and *nahm yum* salad dressings. The juice is sometimes called for in dressings, especially for elegant salads with heritage in Royal Thai cuisine. Whole makrut limes keep well in the freezer, ideal for grating or peeling the desired amount of zest when needed. Unfortunately, though, freezing the fruit renders the juice very bitter and unappetising. Makrut lime leaves are used extensively in Thai cuisine, added whole to soups, braises and curries to release their wonderful perfume, or finely shredded in salads and garnishes. If you can find fresh leaves, then this will give the best flavour; failing that, Asian supermarkets (grocery stores) have frozen leaves available in the freezer section, where they will keep well for months. Don't bother with the dried leaves, as these will have lost all their bright citrus flavour.

Long chillies • *prik chi faa*
These are about 10 cm (4 in) in length and grown in various colours, although red and green are the most common varieties available. Red chillies have a fuller, richer flavour compared to their green counterparts. Long chillies are very versatile. When preparing them, the seeds should be removed to dampen the chillies' fierce heat without compromising their fruity, spicy flavour.

Bird's eye chillies • *prik kii nuu suan*

The quintessential Thai chilli with a memorable spice level. They are widely used in their green form throughout Thailand, where the slightly unripe chillies have a sharp, viciously hot flavour that can be fiercely addictive. In the UK, they are far more commonly found in their ripe red form, but these are equally delicious in all varieties of Thai dishes. These chillies are affectionately known as 'mouse shits' among Thai chefs I have worked with, as their name translates to 'rat dropping chilli' due to their size and the sometimes surprising spicy heat they bring to a dish. Remove the stems and keep in a container in the freezer.

Coriander root • *pak chi raak*

Unlike in Western culture, the root of the coriander (cilantro) plant is highly prized in Thailand, where it is used extensively in *nahm jim* dipping sauces, curry pastes and marinades. It can be found in Asian supermarkets (grocery stores) and freezes well. Failing that, coriander stems can be used as a substitute when a recipe calls for the root.

Lemongrass • *dtakrai*

These long, fibrous stalks have an intense citrus flavour, and are used in curry pastes, salads and soups. Any surplus lemongrass can be prepared (see Knife Techniques on page 27) and finely shredded, then stored in the freezer for pounding into curry pastes, although I wouldn't recommend using frozen and thawed lemongrass for other dishes, such as salads and soups.

Fingerroot • *krachai*

Made up of a cluster of long, spindly 'fingers' attached at their base by a dense root, peeling their thin brown skin releases the fragrant, earthy and peppery flavour. They are used widely in fish and seafood dishes, as well as the famous jungle curry (*gaeng ba*) of rural Thailand. Once peeled, *krachai* can be stored in the freezer, but can only really be used for pounding into curry pastes once thawed.

Galangal • *khaa*

Part of the rhizome root family, along with ginger, turmeric and fingerroot, galangal shares many attributes with ginger, except that it has an almost citrussy medicinal flavour that is reminiscent of pine. Young galangal has a thin white skin with pink sprouts that can be used in soups or thinly shredded into salads. As galangal matures, the skin thickens and the flavour intensifies, becoming more pungent and peppery. Mature galangal is favoured for robustly flavoured curry pastes, whereas younger roots are used in salads and soups. Peeled galangal can be portioned and stored in the freezer for up to six months to great effect.

Turmeric • *kamin*

Another rhizome in the same tuber family as galangal and *krachai*. Several varieties are available throughout Thailand, but it's rare to find anything but the deep orange-fleshed roots on British shores. The fresh root has a strong medicinal aroma and vibrant, bright flavour compared with ground turmeric, which tends to be musty and bitter. Fresh turmeric is heavily used in Southern Thailand and stores well, peeled and portioned, for up to six months in the freezer. Not commonly found outside of Thailand, but worth mentioning nonetheless, is white turmeric (*kamin kao*), which has a crisp and juicy flesh that complements richer dishes and can be eaten raw. A truly intriguing ingredient.

Coconut • *mapraow*

Fresh coconut can be eaten in many stages of its life. The younger coconuts (*mapraow orn*) have thirst-quenching water with life-giving properties if you're suffering from a hangover! The soft, almost jelly-like flesh can be used in sweet and savoury dishes, giving a subtle nutty flavour and gelatinous texture. Older brown coconuts are prized for making fresh coconut cream, and their harder flesh is shredded and toasted to give a fragrant, nutty flavour to dishes. There are also teenage coconuts (*mapraow teun teuk*) available in Thailand: these aren't quite as mature as the older brown nuts, and so the flesh is tender and can be used fresh in desserts and salads.

Thai basil • *bai horapha*

This fragrant leaf is pungent and has an aniseedy, almost liquorice flavour. The leaves are used to sweeten and perfume dishes from curries to soups and salads. The purple stems are not edible, but are useful for adding fragrance to stocks, braises and liquid brines. Flowering buds can be picked separately from the leaves to be pounded into pastes for curries and stir-fries.

Holy basil • *bai grapao*
This basil is very different to its Thai basil counterpart, with a fragrance comparable to dried cloves. This slightly jagged green leaf is indispensable when making the famous Bangkok street dish *pad grapao* (meat stir-fried with holy basil) – for my version, see page 122.

Wild pepper leaf • *bai cha plu*
This is commonly used throughout the Thai Kingdom for 'One-bite' Royal Snack (*miang kham*) (page 168) as the vessel for carrying ingredients and flavours. It is otherwise referred to as *betel*, but should not be confused with the tough, thick leaf used for Indian *paan*, a snack chewed for its caffeine-like stimulant effects. The taste of *bai cha plu* is slightly peppery, so I grow nasturtium plants in my garden and let the leaves grow larger before picking them to use as an Anglo alternative in my dishes.

Sawtooth coriander • *pak chi farang*
Sometimes called long-leaf coriander (cilantro) or sold as *ngò gai* in Vietnamese markets. As the name suggests, the leaves are long (about 20 cm/8 in), with jagged and serrated 'sawtooth' edges. It has a taste not too dissimilar to regular coriander. Britain has a native coastal herb called sea arrowgrass that makes a wonderful substitute if you live near the coast and like to forage; otherwise, regular coriander works fine.

Hot mint • *phak pai*
Otherwise known as Vietnamese coriander and labelled *rau răm* in Vietnamese markets, these slender and pointed leaves are slightly variegated with a hot flavour that is reminiscent of both coriander (cilantro) and mint. It is widely eaten with *laab* (chopped meat) in Northern and Northeastern Thailand. I have yet to find a direct substitute in the British larder. Instead, I have a hardy bush of Vietnamese hot mint growing in my garden that I can pick leaves from when required. Look online for infant plants if you want to do something similar at home.

Pandan leaf • *bai dtoei hom*
Often described as Asia's vanilla pod (bean), pandan is used in Thai sweets to flavour coconut cream and sugar syrups. I find it has gentle nutty tones and a background 'green' flavour. The leaves are long and slender, and are often knotted and thrown in with rice as it steams to give a lovely aroma. It is widely available in Asian stores and normally sold in bunches. I knot the leaves individually, then keep them in an airtight container in the freezer for up to six months for easy use at home.

Equipment

When cooking Thai food, some of the equipment and techniques required might feel slightly archaic and old-fashioned, but, as the saying goes, 'if it ain't broke, don't fix it'. Below is a list of equipment I use at home, ranging from essential to useful depending on how much Thai cooking you are planning to undertake. That being said, a modern Thai kitchen is virtually indistinguishable from a traditional Western kitchen, with plenty of overlap in the equipment used. To make your life easier, only a few specialist items are required in order to produce the Thai dishes I've shared here.

Pestle and mortar

The pestle and mortar is the most indispensable piece of kit in a Thai kitchen: no Thai home is without one. I use mine daily, and once you invest in a quality pestle and mortar, I bet you will too. The most loyal, reliable and hard-working are made from stone, usually granite, and are larger than anything we are used to in Western kitchens. The larger the better, as this will make them more efficient and versatile. I recommend buying a stone mortar with an opening around 25 cm (10 in) in diameter. This will accommodate all manner of uses, from pounding curry pastes and *nahm jim* sauces, to grinding toasted spices and milling toasted rice into a powder for Isaan dishes, or simply breaking up and bruising ingredients prior to infusing in soups and braises. The invention of the food processor has certainly made kitchen tasks more convenient and quicker, but in principle this modern gadget does not perform the same task as the humble pestle and mortar. The main difference is a food processor cuts and tears ingredients, which can cause discoloration. The action of pounding a heavy stone pestle into a deep, wide-mouthed mortar causes the ingredients to be crushed and pulverised, melding their flavours together. The other main issue with using a food processor when making curry paste is that, without the addition of liquid (usually water or oil), the ingredients will not purée and blend sufficiently into a smooth paste. Additional liquid is not required when using a pestle and mortar, and so the finished paste will be more concentrated in flavour, with the ingredients married together in a harmonious paste. In Thai culture, people believe that the true character of each cook is revealed when using a pestle and mortar. A regular and rhythmical pounding indicates the person is of an even and consistent temperament, showing patience and discipline, rather than an irregular style with an abrupt stop-start technique. Something to consider when you first start to master using the *pok pok*, a nickname that has been coined for the pestle and mortar due to the sound made as the pestle connects with the mortar. American chef Andy Ricker affectionately called his Portland based restaurant Pok Pok in tribute to this modest but essential tool.

Clay mortar and wooden pestle

The most ancient versions of the mortar (bowl-shaped chamber) was made from clay with the pestle (stick) made from wood. Today this style of mortar and pestle is still widely used in the Thai kitchen, mostly favoured for making salads such as the famous pounded green papaya salad (*som tam*). They can be purchased online. If you are looking to invest, be sure to buy a clay mortar with an opening of around 20 cm (8 in) in diameter. Soak the clay mortar in a bucket of cold water overnight before using it for the first time. This will prevent it shattering during use.

Wok

No Asian kitchen is complete without a wok – not just for stir-frying, but also deep-frying, boiling, toasting spices and steaming. You don't need to invest lots of money to get a decent wok these days. The style you buy will be dependent on the style of your kitchen hob; a flat-bottomed, carbon-steel wok will suit most people with a conventional gas hob like the one I have at home. The relatively thin material heats quickly and retains hot temperatures, which is ideal for rapid stir-fry cooking. Take a look at your local homeware store or search online for something with relatively steep sides, as this conical shape will funnel the food into the centre of the wok, where the temperature is at its hottest. As a tip, before I use my wok I place it over the highest heat for a few minutes to burn any residual grease off the surface, giving a clean cooking surface. As the wok heats up, it will probably start to smoke and smell, but after a few minutes, this will have dissipated. At this point, you can either add a glug of oil for fast, high-temperature cooking, or you can add some cold water to cool the surface. Simply tip the water out and wipe the surface clean, then you will be ready to cook.

Spider strainer

This is otherwise known as bird's nest strainer or long-handled strainer, due to the shape of the straining nest and the long bamboo handle. It is an indispensable utensil when wok cooking. It's great for deep-frying, poaching or boiling, allowing you to gather large amounts of items without straining the entire contents of a wok. These strainers are very affordable and easy to find online or in Asian stores and grocers.

Heavy cleaver

I have a few cleavers at home, but the most useful are the heavy, dull kind that are ideal for cracking hard objects like coconut husks and cutting through chicken bones or fish bodies. I favour a cleaver when breaking down lots of fibrous lemongrass and galangal for curry pastes, as these hardy ingredients can blunt your chef's knife in no time. Look to buy one from an Asian store, and choose the basic, cheap sort that can take a battering.

Digital scales

Not specialist to an Asian kitchen, but a very handy piece of equipment for everyday cooking. A set of digital scales will be useful each and every time you cook, regardless of the cuisine. If you get accustomed to metric weight measurements, your cooking will be more exact and consistent.

Electric rice cooker

Not essential (you can achieve perfectly boiled rice using a pan and lid, see page 195), but an electric rice cooker will not only make your life easier, it will also free up hob space in small home kitchens and will almost certainly result in a more consistent final product.

Bamboo steamer

This doesn't have to be bamboo, but I mention it as these steamers are incredibly cheap to buy from Asian stores and, depending on how many you are cooking for, you can keep stacking them up to accommodate more portions. At home, I have 20 cm (8 in) and 25 cm (10 in) diameter baskets, as they fit conveniently in my wok and allow for enough water underneath to let ingredients steam perfectly.

Japanese mandolin

Not essential, but since I bought my first Japanese mandolin I don't know what I did without one. The blade is razor sharp (watch those fingers!) and they come with various blade attachments for cutting vegetables into different thicknesses and lengths. Particularly good for cutting large quantities into equal-size matchsticks (like for *som tam*) or slicing vegetables wafer-thin.

Spice grinder

Once again, not essential, but I use my spice grinder regularly as I find the flavour of freshly toasted and ground spices far superior to shop-bought ground spices. If you buy whole spices and keep them in airtight containers, this gives you the flexibility to toast and grind what you need. Not only will this result in a better taste, but in the long run, it will also save you money. Personally, I find the process of toasting and grinding spices therapeutic, and I love the aroma given off by freshly toasted spices. As a rule, you want to heat the spices in a dry pan over a low–medium heat for a few minutes until they begin to crackle and colour, releasing their lovely fragrance. Leave them to cool before grinding as finely as possible, and then pass the powder through a sieve (fine-mesh strainer) to remove any larger pieces. Keep the ground spices in an airtight container, preferably in the refrigerator to extend freshness. The grinding of dry spices to a powder can be achieved in a large stone pestle and mortar, but this is a little more time consuming and involves some elbow grease!

yum / laab

Salads and 'Laab'

Salads are some of the most interesting and diverse dishes in the Thai repertoire. They hold very few similarities to the vinaigrette-dressed green lettuce leaves we associate with Western salads, and in contrast are packed with aromatic herbs and intensely vibrant dressings made by pounding chillies and garlic with sugar, lime juice and fish sauce. On occasion, roasted chilli jam (*nahm prik pao*) or coconut cream are used to give richness and body to Thai dressings, while other elements, such as fried shallots and garlic, or roasted coconut and toasted rice powder, provide contrast in texture. It's worth noting that although *yum* widely translates to 'salad', it actually means to mix or toss ingredients together. Many of the salads in this chapter can be enjoyed as a light meal, accompanied by the obligatory bowl of steamed jasmine rice or a few coils of *khanom jim* (rice vermicelli noodles), but can sit equally well among a range of dishes as part of a wider meal. I have included a recipe for Northern Thai *laab* (Thai Steak Tartare) and its Isaan cousin Citrus-cured Tuna (*koi*). Both dishes are centred around a protein that is mixed with a dressing, herbs and other aromatic ingredients, much like the other Thai salads included in this chapter.

yum khai dao

Fried Egg Salad

This salad is not commonly found in Thai restaurants, but it is incredibly easy to cook at home. At its core, eggs are cracked into smoking-hot oil and shallow-fried so that the edges and bottom get crispy, the whites puff out, yet the yolk remains runny and molten. It's traditionally paired with Asian celery, but regular celery works just fine. The salad is tossed in a sweet, spicy and tart dressing that's both moreish and satisfying, showcasing how even the simplest of Thai dishes can achieve complex flavours.

SERVES 2

2 large eggs
vegetable oil, for shallow-frying
½ small white onion, thinly sliced with the grain of the onion (from top to tail)
1 salad tomato, chopped into 8 pieces
2 sticks celery, stalk thinly sliced and leaves picked (use the paler inner stalks of a celery head with the leaves)
3 tablespoons roughly chopped coriander (cilantro) sprigs

For the salad dressing *(nahm yum)*

2 tablespoons palm or brown sugar
1 tablespoon water
3 tablespoons fish sauce
3 tablespoons lime juice
1 teaspoon thinly sliced garlic
2 bird's eye chillies, thinly sliced

To make the dressing, mix together the sugar, water, fish sauce and lime juice in a pestle and mortar until the sugar has completely dissolved. Add the garlic and chillies and stir through, then set aside. It will taste spicy, sweet and tart.

Crack the eggs into separate ramekins or small bowls, taking care not to break the yolks. Pour the oil for shallow-frying into a shallow saucepan to a depth of 2 cm (¾ in) and heat over a high heat. Once the oil starts to smoke, gently slide an egg into the hot oil. The egg will immediately start to spit, crackle and bubble, so be very careful. The egg white will puff up and develop large, transparent bubbles, and the bottom and edges will get brown and crispy. Fry for about 1 minute, then flip the egg over and cook for a few seconds on the other side before transferring to a plate lined with paper towels to drain the excess oil. Repeat with the second egg.

Cut the fried eggs into bite-size quarters, trying to avoid cutting directly through the runny yolks, and arrange on a serving plate. In a large bowl, gently toss together the sliced onion, tomato, celery and coriander with the dressing until combined. Top the eggs with the salad and dressing and serve.

yum makhua yao
Smoky Aubergine Salad with Soft-boiled Egg

Traditionally, this salad, which hails from Isaan, is made using long green aubergines (eggplants). These specific aubergines are hard to come by on British shores so I look out for the long purple aubergines (known as Japanese aubergines) that are sometimes available, but you can also make this salad using the widely available regular Italian aubergines. The aubergines become smoky and luxurious by barbecuing (grilling) over hot coals, but you can replicate this effect by charring them over your gas hob or under a hot grill (broiler). Just be sure to cook them directly over a very high heat to blacken and blister their skins while keeping the insides moist and juicy.

SERVES 2

4 tablespoons dried shrimp (omit if making a vegetarian/vegan version)
1 large egg, at room temperature
2 long purple Japanese aubergines (eggplants) or 1 regular Italian aubergine
½ small red onion, thinly sliced with the grain of the onion
2 makrut lime leaves (fresh or frozen), finely shredded
4 tablespoons coriander (cilantro) leaves
3 tablespoons mint leaves

For the salad dressing (*nahm yum*)

2 tablespoons palm sugar
1 tablespoon water
1½ tablespoons fish sauce (or use thin light soy sauce for a vegetarian/vegan version)
2 tablespoons lime juice
1 teaspoon Toasted Chilli Powder (*prik bon*) (page 213)

Light a charcoal grill or preheat an indoor grill (broiler), if using.

To make the dressing, mix all the ingredients together in a pestle and mortar until the sugar has completely dissolved. It will taste spicy, sweet and sour with a salty finish. Set aside.

To prepare the shrimp, if using, pound the dried shrimp in a stone pestle and mortar until a floss-like texture is achieved. Alternatively, use a spice grinder or small food processor to achieve a light flossed texture. Store in an airtight container in the refrigerator for up to two weeks if making a larger quantity.

Bring a small saucepan of water to the boil and cook the egg to your liking. I prefer an egg with a fudgy yolk, so I boil mine for 6 minutes before plunging it into a bowl of iced water. Once cool enough to handle, peel the egg and set aside for later.

Barbecue (grill) the aubergines over hot coals, or over the highest flame on your hob, or under a very hot grill. The skins need to be completely blackened so the flesh inside becomes soft and tender with a smoky flavour. Leave until cool enough to handle, then peel off the blackened skins and discard. Roughly chop the aubergine flesh while still warm and arrange on a serving plate.

Combine the sliced onion, makrut lime leaves, coriander and mint in a medium bowl with the dressing. Gently toss the salad together and arrange over the aubergine, then pour over any remaining dressing. Halve the soft-boiled egg and place on top of the salad. Finish by generously sprinkling with the shrimp floss.

SERVE WITH

- Steamed Sticky Rice (*khao neow*) (page 196)
- Chiang Mai Herbal Sausage (*sai ua*) (page 70)
- Burmese Pork Belly Curry with Pickled Garlic (*gaeng hung lae*) (page 144)

yum aepbpeern

Green Apple and Crispy Dried Anchovy Salad

This salad makes use of fruits in their unripe stage of growth, much like the beloved green papaya salad (*som tam*) that is widely eaten throughout Thailand. This particular salad commonly uses green mango, but I've opted to use green apple, as I find varieties like Granny Smith offer the same crisp texture and sweet-tart flavour as a green mango.

SERVES 2

120 ml (4 fl oz/½ cup) vegetable oil, for deep-frying
2 tablespoons dried anchovies or dried shrimp
2 tablespoons raw peanuts, preferably skin-on
8 makrut lime leaves (fresh or frozen), 6 left whole and 2 finely shredded
juice of ½ lime
2 green apples, such as Granny Smith
½ small red onion, thinly sliced with the grain of the onion
2 lemongrass stalks, root and outer husks removed, thinly sliced
1 long red chilli, seeded and finely shredded
3 tablespoons coriander (cilantro) leaves
2 tablespoons mint leaves

For the salad dressing (nahm yum)

1 long red chilli, seeded and chopped
2 red bird's eye chillies, chopped
1 tablespoon chopped coriander (cilantro) root or coriander stem
1 tablespoon chopped garlic
½ teaspoon salt
1 teaspoon palm or brown sugar
3 tablespoons lime juice
2 tablespoons fish sauce

To make the salad dressing, pound the chillies, coriander root, garlic and salt together in a stone pestle and mortar to a smooth paste. Add the sugar and mix until well combined. Finish by stirring in the lime juice and fish sauce. It will taste spicy, salty and sour. Set aside.

Heat the oil for deep-frying in a large, deep saucepan until the oil reaches 180°C (350°F) on a cooking thermometer. Alternatively, drop a small cube of bread into the hot oil; if it turns golden brown in about 15 seconds, the oil is ready. Carefully drop the dried anchovies or shrimp into the oil and, using a slotted spoon or spatula, move around in the pan for 15 seconds, or until golden and crispy. Remove and leave to drain on a plate lined with paper towels to remove the excess oil.

Reheat the oil to 180°C (350°F) and repeat the process with the peanuts, then the six whole makrut lime leaves, being careful with the lime leaves as they will spit and sputter as they hit the hot oil. Again, drain on a plate lined with paper towels.

Fill a medium bowl with cold water and add the lime juice. Cut the apple into long strands using a Japanese mandolin set with 3 mm (⅛ in) teeth (alternatively, you can do this by hand). The strands should be about 6 cm (2½ in) long and 3 mm (⅛ in) wide. Add the apple strands to the acidulated water as you go to prevent them oxidising and turning an unattractive brown colour while you cut the remaining apple.

Drain the apple strands well, then add to a large bowl, along with all the other ingredients except the crispy fried makrut lime leaves. Add the red chilli dressing and toss together to ensure the salad is nicely coated. Spoon on to a serving plate and garnish with the crispy makrut lime leaves to serve.

yum galam bplee

Sweetheart Cabbage, Roast Chicken and Chilli Jam Salad

This recipe came about when I was thinking about an alternative to banana blossom salad (*yum hua plee*). I find banana blossoms have a gentle flavour, not too dissimilar to cabbage or artichoke, with a snappy texture that holds up well to being cooked. I'm also a big fan of sweetheart cabbage (sometimes called hispi cabbage) and decided it would make a great substitute in this style of salad, especially when paired with grilled or roast chicken and an umami-rich chilli jam dressing.

SERVES 2

1 brown coconut
200 g (7 oz) sweetheart cabbage (about ½ cabbage)
½ teaspoon salt
120 g (4 oz) leftover roast chicken, skin removed (a mix of white and dark meat)
3 lemongrass stalks, root and outer husks removed, thinly sliced
½ small red onion, thinly sliced with the grain of the onion
3 tablespoons Thai basil leaves
3 tablespoons coriander (cilantro) leaves
2 tablespoons mint leaves
2 tablespoons nasturtium leaves or wild pepper leaves, roughly torn (optional)
2 dried long chillies, seeded and deep-fried in oil until crispy
1 tablespoon Fried Shallots (*hom jiaw*) (page 210)
1 tbsp Fried Garlic (*gratiam jiaw*) (page 211)
2 makrut lime leaves (fresh or frozen), thinly shredded
2 tablespoons coconut cream

For the salad dressing (*nahm yum*)

6 tablespoons Roasted Chilli Jam (*nahm prik pao*) (page 82)
4 tablespoons coconut cream
2 makrut lime leaves (fresh or frozen)
1 lemongrass stalk, cut into 5 cm (2 in) batons and bruised in a pestle and mortar
1 tablespoon palm or brown sugar
1 teaspoon Tamarind Water (*nahm makham piak*) (page 214)
1 teaspoon fish sauce
2 tablespoons mandarin or clementine juice

For the salad dressing, gently warm the Roasted Chilli Jam and coconut cream together in a saucepan over a low heat for 1 minute. Add the makrut lime leaves and lemongrass batons and simmer gently for 2 minutes, making sure the jam doesn't catch on the base of the pan. Add the sugar, Tamarind Water, fish sauce and mandarin or clementine juice and simmer for another minute. It will taste rich and sweet, slightly salty and spicy, with a sheen of oil on the surface. This will make more dressing than required, but it will keep well in an airtight container in the refrigerator for up to a month. Leave to cool to just above room temperature.

For the roasted coconut, crack the brown coconut (page 208) and shred the flesh using a regular box grater. Add to a wok or saucepan and toast over a low heat for 5 minutes until the coconut is golden brown and dried with a lovely nutty aroma. Leave to cool. This can be stored in an airtight container for up to a month.

Preheat the oven to 180°C (350°F/gas 4). Sprinkle the salt over the cabbage and wrap it tightly in kitchen foil. Place in the oven for 8 minutes. Check the cabbage after this time: it should be steaming and roasting in its own juices, producing a tender vegetable that retains a slight bite. Remove the foil and leave to cool to just above room temperature before slicing into bite-size pieces.

Flake the leftover chicken into bite-size pieces and place on a baking tray (pan), then transfer to the oven for 5 minutes to warm through.

Add the cabbage, chicken, lemongrass, red onion, herbs and nasturtium leaves to a large bowl. Drizzle with the dressing and toss everything together until well coated but not flooded with the dressing. Crumble the fried dried chilli over the salad, along with half the Fried Shallots and Fried Garlic. Toss together, then pile on to a large serving plate. Finish by scattering over the remaining Fried Shallots and Fried Garlic, along with the shredded makrut lime leaves. Drizzle with the coconut cream and serve.

som tam farang

Shredded Vegetables with Spicy-sweet-sour-salty Dressing

This recipe is influenced by a classic dish in the Thai cooking repertoire – green papaya salad (*som tam*). Every person in Thailand eats *som tam*; it's as widely eaten as a Sunday roast is in Britain, and similarly everyone has a preference on how it should be made and what ingredients should be present or omitted. *Som tam* is a salad of unripe green papaya that is pounded and muddled with a dressing of chillies and garlic (spicy), palm sugar (sweet), tamarind and lime juice (sour) and fish sauce or fermented fish sauce (salty) – although ingredients and quantities are interchangeable depending on personal preference.

SERVES 2

2 bird's eye chillies (add more or less depending on how much spice you can handle)
1 tablespoon chopped garlic
1 tablespoon palm sugar
2 tablespoons Tamarind Water (*nahm makham piak*) (page 214)
2 tablespoons fish sauce or use thin light soy sauce for a vegetarian/vegan version
2 tablespoons lime juice
3 tablespoons (45 g/1½ oz) carrot, thinly shredded into 3 mm (⅛ in) wide, 8 cm (3¼ in) long strips using a Japanese mandolin or by hand
3 tablespoons (45 g/1½ oz) celeriac (celery root), thinly shredded into 2 mm (¹⁄₁₆ in) wide, 8 cm (3¼ in) long strips using a Japanese mandolin or by hand
3 tablespoons (45 g/1½ oz) white cabbage, thinly shredded using a Japanese mandolin or by hand
30 g (1 oz) fine green beans, cut into 3 cm (1¼ in) pieces
30 g (1 oz) cherry tomatoes, halved
1 tablespoon dried shrimp, soaked in water for 5 minutes until tender then drained (omit if making a vegetarian/vegan version)
2 tablespoons roasted peanuts (see method on page 168), preferably skinless

In a large clay pestle and mortar, pound the chillies and garlic together to a rough paste. Add the sugar and continue to pound into a paste. Add the Tamarind Water, fish sauce and lime juice, and stir together well until you have a viscous dressing. It will taste spicy, sweet and sour, with a highly seasoned salty finish.

Add the shredded vegetables, beans, tomatoes and dried shrimp to the mortar. Gently, but with some authority, crush and tumble the ingredients with the dressing. The idea is not only to mix the ingredients together, but to pound them so the cell structures of the vegetables are broken and bruised and they absorb more of the dressing. Once well mixed and pounded together, add the peanuts and mix and tumble together until well combined.

Transfer the salad to a serving dish with all of the dressing. The finished salad is designed to have plenty of the dressing pooling on the plate so you can soak it up with sticky rice.

SERVE WITH

- Steamed Sticky Rice (*khao neow*) (page 196)
- Grilled Coriander and Garlic Chicken (*gai yang*) (page 64)
- Ayutthayae Grilled Native Lobster (*goong yai pao*) (page 74)

koi pla Isaan

Citrus-cured Tuna

Koi involves lightly curing and cooking with the use of citrus, usually lime juice, and is not dissimilar to the *ceviche* found throughout South America. Traditionally, the protein is chopped and incorporated with a sour and spicy dressing, and eaten alongside sticky rice and plenty of fresh herbs. I've opted to use tuna, but salmon or trout would work equally well – just try to source the best-quality and freshest fish you can.

SERVES 2

2 tablespoons fish sauce

3 tablespoons lime juice

1 tablespoon caster (superfine) sugar

1 teaspoon Toasted Chilli Powder
   (*prik bon*) (page 213)

120 g (4 oz) tuna loin or belly, cut into
   2 cm (¾ in) dice

3 lemongrass stalks, root and outer
   husks removed, thinly sliced

½ small red onion, thinly sliced with
   the grain of the onion

1 spring onion (scallion), thinly sliced

3 tablespoons roughly chopped
   coriander (cilantro) sprigs

2 tablespoons mint leaves

1 tablespoon Toasted Rice Powder
   (*khao khua*) (page 212)

TO GARNISH

- 2 dried bird's eye chillies, stems on,
  dry-toasted

- 2 tablespoons salmon or trout roe
  (optional)

In a bowl, mix together the fish sauce, lime juice, sugar and Toasted Chilli Powder, making sure the sugar is completely dissolved. The mixture will taste hot, sour and salty.

In a large bowl, combine the diced tuna, lemongrass, red onion, spring onion, coriander and mint. Toss with the dressing and plate immediately, as the tuna will start to cook as it combines with the acidic lime juice.

Sprinkle the rice powder over the top and garnish with the toasted dried bird's eye chillies and salmon or trout roe, if using.

laab dip neua

Thai Steak Tartare

I'm a huge fan of *laab dip*, a raw minced (ground) meat dish heavy on dried spices that's widely eaten in Northern Thailand. I also love the traditional steak tartare known throughout Western culture. Here, I've combined the two dishes and tinkered with the flavours to create a recipe I describe as Thai Steak Tartare. It's a complex dish that has undergone many changes, but there's usually a version of it on the AngloThai menu.

SERVES 4

10 large dried chillies, stems discarded, seeded
1 tablespoon prickly ash (*makhwaen*) or Sichuan peppercorns
1 tablespoon coriander seeds
1 teaspoon fennel seeds
½ teaspoon black peppercorns
¼ teaspoon cumin seeds
1 star anise
2 cloves
1 lemongrass stalks, root and outer husks removed, thinly sliced
1 teaspoon chopped galangal
60 g (2 oz) banana shallots, chopped
2 tablespoons chopped garlic
½ tablespoon shrimp paste
6 tablespoons rendered beef fat (page 216)
3 tablespoons rapeseed (canola) oil
200 g/7 oz dry-aged beef (sirloin, ribeye or fillet) – dry-aged beef has the richest flavour
3 tablespoons thinly sliced garden sorrel leaves, plus 1 tablespoon to garnish
2 tablespoons thinly sliced spring onion (scallion)
2 tablespoons roughly chopped coriander (cilantro) sprigs
2 tablespoons Fried Shallots (*hom jiaw*) (page 210)
2 tablespoons Fried Garlic (*gratiam jiaw*) (page 211)

Toast the dried chillies in a dry wok over a low heat for 1–2 minutes until charred and fragrant. Leave to cool, then blitz in a spice grinder or grind using a stone pestle and mortar to a fine powder. Set aside.

Combine the dried spices in a pan and dry-toast over a low heat for 1–2 minutes until fragrant. Blitz in a spice grinder or grind to a fine powder using a stone pestle and mortar. Set aside.

Pound the lemongrass and galangal into a fine paste using a stone pestle and mortar. Add the shallots and garlic and again work into a smooth paste. Add the shrimp paste and combine the ingredients. Finally, add the blitzed toasted chilli powder and spice powder and mix to incorporate.

Heat the rendered beef fat and the oil together in a frying pan (skillet) over a low heat. Add the seasoning paste and work it into the fat and oil, stirring constantly. Cook for about 5 minutes, stirring all the while. Once the paste smells fragrant with no rawness, remove from the heat and transfer to a container to cool. Be careful not to over-fry, as the dried spices in the paste will become bitter.

Trim the beef of any sinew and fat, then cut into 1 cm (½ in) slices. (To make the beef easier to slice, you can freeze the meat for 15 minutes beforehand. Allow the beef to come to room temperature for 30 minutes before continuing with the recipe.)

Add the beef to a large bowl, along with the sliced sorrel, spring onion, coriander, half the Fried Shallots and half the Fried Garlic.

Warm 2–3 tablespoons of the seasoning paste over a low heat in a small saucepan for 30 seconds until it is just above room temperature, then add to the bowl and dress the beef. Taste and add more seasoning paste, if necessary. It will taste rich, spicy, complex and very in your face! Transfer to a serving plate and top with the remaining Fried Shallots, Fried Garlic and extra sliced sorrel.

SERVE WITH
• Steamed Sticky Rice (*khao neow*) (page 196)

yang

Grilled

Grilling over fire is one of the oldest cooking methods in Thailand and remains popular to this day, particularly in rural communities, where the jungles and forests provide essential fuel for cooking. I personally love cooking over charcoal and find it imparts essential flavours and fragrances that are key to the success of many Thai dishes. That's not to say the recipes in this chapter can't be cooked using a domestic kitchen grill (broiler) or oven, but the flavours will be different to those achieved when cooking over charcoal. This style of cooking is prevalent in the dishes of Northern and Northeastern Thailand, where the style of dishes is more rustic and stripped back. Despite this, cooks show great versatility in the various ways in which charcoal is used to achieve different results. Long aubergines (eggplants) are cooked directly on red-hot coals to burn and blister their skins while steaming the creamy inner flesh for Smoky Aubergine Salad with Soft-boiled Egg (*yum makhua yao*) (page 48). Chillies, shallots and garlic are charred and blistered in their skins for Grilled Long Chilli Relish (*nahm prik num*) (page 83), while the more conventional grilling of meats and seafood enables the items to absorb a little smoky flavour as they cook. I'm sure most of you have a home barbecue, and chances are it will work great for these recipes. Besides a charcoal grill (barbecue), you should invest in a sturdy pair of grill tongs and a stiff wire brush to clean the grill grates before you cook on them. It might sound obvious, but you will get the best results from a clean and oiled barbecue (grill). Just give it a good scrub and oil the grates using a rag or a few layers of paper towels soaked with vegetable oil.

gai yang

Grilled Coriander and Garlic Chicken

Thai grilled chicken is an absolute delight and, in my opinion, is far superior to other grilled chicken dishes from around the world. The dish hails from Isaan, where barbecuing (grilling) over fire is a main cooking method. However, *gai yang* is eaten in every corner of Thailand, served with green papaya salad (*som tam*) and sticky rice (*khao niaw*). The success of this recipe relies on a few processes, but with some planning ahead it is relatively simple to pull off and is great for sharing with family and friends.

SERVES 4

1 teaspoon white peppercorns
1 teaspoon salt
2 tablespoons chopped coriander (cilantro) root or coriander stem
3 tablespoons chopped garlic
1 tablespoon palm or brown sugar
½ teaspoon ground turmeric
½ teaspoon ground coriander
3 tablespoons fish sauce
1 tablespoon vegetable oil
1 small chicken or poussin, about 450 g (1 lb)
2 tablespoons Sweet Fish Sauce (*nahm pla waan*) (page 114)

SERVE WITH

- Sweet Chilli Sauce (*nahm jim gai waan*) (page 218)
- Sticky Rice (*khao neow*) (page 196)
- Shredded Vegetables with Spicy-sweet-sour Dressing (*som tam farang*) (page 54)

Pound the white peppercorns and salt in a pestle and mortar to a fine powder, then add the coriander root and garlic and pound to a smooth paste. Add the sugar, turmeric, ground coriander, fish sauce and oil, and mix until combined and smooth.

Using a pair of heavy-duty scissors, cut the chicken along the backbone to butterfly (spatchcock) the bird. Place the chicken, breast-side up, on a cutting board. Gently, but with some authority, press down on the chicken using the palm of your hand so that the chicken becomes flattened. This will allow it to cook evenly on your charcoal barbecue (grill).

Rub the marinade all over the chicken, coating it thoroughly, then leave to marinate in the refrigerator for at least 6 hours or overnight.

When ready to cook, prepare a charcoal grill (barbecue), then cook the chicken over a medium heat for 15–20 minutes until cooked through. To do this, start by placing the exposed cavity side of the chicken on the grill and leave for two-thirds of the cooking time; the bones will protect the delicate white flesh from overcooking and becoming dry. Flip the chicken over so that it's breast-side down, and cook for the final one-third of the cooking time to colour the skin a golden brown. Leave the chicken to rest in a warm spot for 5 minutes.

Before serving, use a pastry brush to liberally glaze the chicken with the Sweet Fish Sauce. Transfer to a cutting board and carve into pieces. I would suggest halving the chicken down the middle of the breastbone and removing the legs, then separating the legs and thighs through the joint. Remove the smaller drumsticks and wings, then cut the breast through the bone into 2–3 pieces. Serve with any (or all) of the suggested accompaniments.

lin wua yang

Beef Tongue with Grilled Chilli Relish

There is something incredibly satisfying about using the whole carcass of an animal, letting nothing go to waste. This is not only the most sustainable approach to cooking, but also the most resourceful, and something that Thai cooks are naturally very good at, making delicious food from whatever is available. This recipe transforms the humble beef tongue into a tender and flavourful meat.

SERVES 6

1 kg (2 lb 4 oz) beef tongue
(1 regular tongue)
40 g (1½ oz/⅓ cup) salt, plus
1 tablespoon
1 tablespoon white peppercorns
outer husks and root offcuts of
6 lemongrass stalks, chopped
3 makrut lime leaves (fresh or frozen)
2 tablespoons chopped coriander
(cilantro) root or coriander stem
1 pandan leaf, knotted
1 garlic bulb, halved horizontally
1 small white onion, halved

**For the grilled chilli relish
(*jaew bong*)**

6 dried long chillies, stems discarded
and seeded
½ regular banana shallot (50 g/2 oz),
skin left on
1 large garlic bulb, cloves broken
individually and threaded on to a
bamboo skewer
1 tablespoon thinly sliced galangal,
threaded on to a bamboo skewer
4 cherry tomatoes, threaded on to
a bamboo skewer
1 teaspoon salt
1 teaspoon palm or brown sugar
1 tablespoon fish sauce
1 tablespoon Tamarind Water (*nahm
makham piak*) (page 214)
Toasted Chilli Powder (*prik bon*)
(page 213), optional

Rinse the tongue, then add to a large saucepan and cover with cold water. Add the 1 tablespoon of salt and bring to the boil over a medium heat, then drain the tongue and discard the water. Rinse the tongue again, then clean the pan of any scum. Return the tongue to the pan and cover with 2 litres (70 fl oz/8 cups) of water seasoned with the 40 g (1½ oz/⅓ cup) of salt. Add the peppercorns, lemongrass offcuts, makrut lime leaves, coriander root, pandan leaf, halved garlic and onion. Gently bring to a simmer and cook for 1½–2 hours until a sharp knife comes out of the fattest part of the tongue with no resistance. You may need to add more water as it cooks to keep the tongue covered.

Remove the pan from the heat and leave the tongue to cool to room temperature in the poaching liquor. Once cool, peel the tough outer layer off the tongue and trim away any unsightly and overly fatty parts. Cut the tongue into 2 cm (¾ in) slices, cutting against the length of the tongue.

For the grilled chilli relish, prepare a charcoal grill (barbecue) and allow the charcoal to burn down to a medium heat with no flame. Grill the dried long chillies until dark, brittle and smoky. Add the shallot and garlic to the grill, still in their skins, and cook for 10–15 minutes until completely soft, then remove and discard the skins. Add the galangal to the grill and cook until dried and fragrant, then add the tomatoes and grill until charred and blistered.

Pound the grilled chillies and the salt in a pestle and mortar to a fine powder. Chop the grilled galangal, shallot and garlic, then pound into the chilli powder until you have a smooth paste. Add the tomatoes and mash them into the paste until a slightly rustic and chunky relish is achieved. Add the sugar, fish sauce and Tamarind Water. Adjust the seasoning as necessary, adding some Toasted Chilli Powder if it needs more heat.

Stoke up your fire with more charcoal, then grill the tongue over a high heat to warm it through and give a charred and smoky flavour. Cut each slice on the diagonal so that you have two bite-size triangular pieces. Serve with the grilled chilli relish.

SERVE WITH
• Steamed Sticky Rice (*khao neow*) (page 196)

neua yang nahm tok

Grilled Beef Ribeye with 'Waterfall' Salad

Nahm tok is an Isaan dish that has all the typical flavour characteristics of the region – spicy, herbal, sour and salty. The name *nahm tok* literally translates as 'waterfall' and receives its whimsical name from the grilling meat juices dripping and falling on to the hot coals as the steak cooks. This process creates smoke and imparts a wonderful flavour. This recipe works best with dry-aged cuts with a good fat marbling, such as ribeye and sirloin.

SERVES 2

2 tablespoons fish sauce
1 tablespoon seasoning sauce (see page 32)
½ teaspoon caster (superfine) sugar
½ tsp ground white pepper
450 g (1 lb) ribeye steak, preferably on the bone and dry-aged for at least 21 days
3 tablespoons coriander (cilantro) leaves
2 tablespoons mint leaves
1 spring onion (scallion), thinly sliced
½ small red onion, thinly sliced with the grain of the onion
2 lemongrass stalks, root and outer husks removed, thinly sliced
2 makrut lime leaves (fresh or frozen), thinly shredded
2 dried bird's eye chillies, toasted (optional)
1 tablespoon Toasted Rice Powder (*khao khua*) (page 212)

For the dressing (*nahm yum*)
4 tablespoons lime juice
2½ tablespoons fish sauce
1½ tablespoons caster (superfine) sugar
1 teaspoon Toasted Chilli Powder (*prik bon*) (page 213)

For the dressing, mix together the lime juice, fish sauce, sugar and Toasted Chilli Powder in a small bowl. This should taste aggressively sour, spicy and salty. Set aside at room temperature until later.

In another small bowl, mix together the fish sauce, seasoning sauce, sugar and white pepper. Rub this all over the steak and leave to marinate for 1 hour in the refrigerator.

Prepare a charcoal grill, then cook the steak over a medium heat, turning once or twice, to give nice caramelisation and colour. I recommend cooking ribeye to medium, but cook to your preference. Leave the steak to rest for at least 5 minutes, before slicing against the grain of the meat.

In a medium bowl, mix together the coriander, mint, spring onion, red onion, lemongrass, makrut lime leaf and toasted dried chillies until combined. Add enough of the dressing to nicely coat the herbs and aromatics without drowning the leaves, then toss everything together gently to coat.

Arrange the sliced steak on a serving plate and pour over a little of the dressing to season. Arrange the herbal salad over the top of the steak and finish with a generous sprinkle of the Toasted Rice Powder to serve.

sai ua

Chiang Mai Herbal Sausage

This has to be one of the tastiest sausages I have ever tried, if not *the* tastiest! I first encountered *sai ua* on a trip to Chiang Mai, where large spiral coils of the sausage are widely sold at markets. The pork sausages were slow-grilling over charcoal and coconut husks, which imparted a wonderful flavour. Traditional versions of this sausage are loose-textured and explode with bright, aromatic flavours of curry paste, herbs and spices, but the best versions are rich and juicy from the addition of hand-chopped pork back fat. Ask your local butcher about spool sausage casings, as they will be able to get these for you.

SERVES 8

1 spool sausage (hog) casing, about 1.5 m (5 ft) long and 2.5 cm (1 in) diameter
1 tablespoon white wine vinegar
300 g (10½ oz) pork shoulder, roughly minced (ground) by your butcher
300 g (10½ oz) pork belly, roughly minced by your butcher
50 g (2 oz) pork back fat, roughly chopped by hand (optional)
1 tablespoon mild curry powder or use madras curry powder
2 tablespoons fish sauce
1 tablespoon light soy sauce
1 tablespoon palm or brown sugar
1 tablespoon makrut lime leaves (fresh or frozen), thinly shredded
8 tablespoons roughly chopped coriander (cilantro) sprigs
8 tablespoons Coconut Smoke Mix (page 209), optional

If the sausage casing comes packed in salt or brine (which they often do), then rinse it thoroughly under cold water, ensuring you run cold water through the inside of the casing as well. This will clean the casing and will allow you to identify any rips or tears. If there are any, then cut out those sections to avoid drama later in the process. Fill a large bowl with water and add the white vinegar. Place the casing in the bowl and leave to soak overnight – this will help the skin to loosen for stuffing.

The next day, pound all the ingredients for the curry paste in a stone pestle and mortar until very smooth. (See pages 204–207 for an expanded explanation on efficiently pounding a curry paste.) Set aside.

Combine all the meat and back fat in a large bowl, then add the curry paste, mild curry powder, fish sauce, soy sauce, sugar and chopped herbs. Use your hands to mix everything together, ensuring each ingredient is well distributed. Test the seasoning by frying a small amount of the mixture in oil and tasting; it should be spicy, salty and herbal.

Tie one end of the sausage casing, then fill it with the mixture, ensuring no air pockets are trapped. The easiest and cheapest way to do this is to fill a large piping bag with the meat mixture, then pipe this directly into the sausage casing. Coil the sausage into a spiral and leave uncovered overnight on a wire rack in the refrigerator to dry out slightly.

For the curry paste
(*khreuang gaeng*)

12 dried long red chillies, seeded and soaked in cold water until soft
1 teaspoon salt
2 tablespoons thinly sliced lemongrass
1 tablespoon chopped galangal
2 tablespoons chopped banana shallot
2 tablespoons chopped garlic
1 tablespoon chopped turmeric root or ½ tablespoon ground turmeric
1 teaspoon shrimp paste
½ teaspoon coriander seeds, briefly toasted and ground into fine powder
½ teaspoon white peppercorns, ground into fine powder

The next day, prepare a charcoal barbecue (grill), then slowly cook the sausage spiral over a medium–low heat for about 30 minutes, or until cooked through, flipping once during cooking. Scatter the hot coals with the Coconut Smoke Mix, if using, to produce a fragrant scented smoke that will flavour the sausage as it cooks. The end result will be an attractively golden amber sausage with a background coconut smoke flavour. Alternatively, roast, grill (broil) or fry the sausage. Leave the sausage to cool for 5 minutes before slicing into 2.5 cm (1 in) pieces to serve.

SERVE WITH
- Grilled Long Chilli Relish (*nahm prik num*) (page 83)
- Pork Scratchings (*khaep mu*) (page 91)
- Sticky Rice (*khao neow*) (page 196)

Chiang Mai Herbal Sausage with Grilled Long Chilli Relish (page 83) and Pork Scratchings (page 91)

goong yai pao
Ayutthaya Grilled Native Lobster

Ayutthaya was the ancient former capital city of Thailand long before Bangkok became the capital in 1782. The province is best known for its historical temples and freshwater rivers and canals, with the latter boasting some of the best freshwater jumbo river prawns (shrimp) in the country. Restaurants dotted along the river banks in this region specialise in serving these jumbo prawns, simply barbecued (grilled) over charcoal and paired with a super spicy seafood dipping sauce (*nahm jim talay*). These massive river prawns are not too dissimiliar to the wonderful native lobsters we catch here in the UK, which is why I have chosen to use the latter in this recipe.

SERVES 4

2 native lobsters, about 600–750 g
(1 lb 5 oz –1 lb 10 oz) each
3 tablespoons rendered pork fat
(page 216) or vegetable oil
1 tablespoon fish sauce
½ teaspoon palm or brown sugar

For the spicy seafood sauce (*nahm jim talay*)
8 bird's eye chillies, chopped
3 tablespoons chopped garlic
1 tablespoon chopped coriander
(cilantro) root or coriander stem
1 teaspoon salt
5 tablespoons lime juice
3 tablespoons fish sauce
1 tablespoon water
1 tablespoon palm or caster
(superfine) sugar

For the spicy seafood sauce, pound the chillies, garlic, coriander root and salt in a pestle and mortar to a smooth paste. Add the lime juice, fish sauce, water and sugar and mix everything together until the sugar has completely dissolved and the ingredients are well combined. It will taste very spicy and sour-salty. Set aside.

Humanely kill the lobster by placing it in the freezer for 10 minutes to sedate. Set the lobster on a cutting board and locate the cross or X at the top of the lobster's head; about 2.5 cm (1 in) above its eyes. Insert the tip of a sharp knife into the cross and cut through the head, then continue cutting through the tail to split the entire lobster. Don't worry if the lobster's legs move for a little while after it's been killed; these are involuntary reflexes, but can be a little alarming.

Remove and discard the small sand sac at the base of the head just behind the eyes, as well as the dark-veined digestive tract running along the centre of the tail. If you prefer, you can remove and discard the light green tomalley (liver and pancreas) in the lobster head – although this is edible and delicious! Crack the claws with the back of a heavy knife.

Warm the rendered pork fat or oil in a saucepan over a low heat, stirring in the fish sauce and sugar to create a flavoured fat with which to baste the lobster during cooking.

Prepare a charcoal grill, then place the lobsters, shell-side down, on the grill rack and cook for 5 minutes until the shells turn bright red. Using a pastry brush, baste the lobster flesh and cracked claws with the flavoured pork fat, then flip the lobster over and cook for another 5 minutes until the flesh is firm, opaque and easily prises away from the shell. Baste the lobster meat and claws again, then leave to rest for a few minutes before serving with the spicy seafood sauce for dipping.

SERVE WITH
- Steamed Sticky Rice (*khao neow*) (page 196)
- Green Apple and Crispy Dried Anchovy Salad (*yum aepbpeern*) (page 51)
- Fragrant Shrimp and Coconut Cream Relish (*lon gapi*) (page 86)
- Deep-fried Vegetables (*pak tort*) (page 89)

yang

pla pao

Whole Salt-crusted Sea Bass

A whole fish encased in salt crust and grilling over charcoal is one of the most alluring sights you will see when browsing the street markets of Northern Thailand. It's a relatively simple preparation and rustic cooking style, but the results are magnificent. Not only does the salt crust protect the delicate flesh of the fish, keeping it juicy and tender during the cooking process, but it also ensures the fish is beautifully seasoned throughout. Tilapia is the favoured fish for this preparation in Thailand, but I opt for widely available sea bass or bream.

SERVES 4

1 whole sea bass, scaled and gutted, about 600 g (1 lb 5 oz)
4–6 herb sprigs, such as coriander (cilantro), Thai basil and hot mint
2 lemongrass stalks, bruised
4 makrut lime leaves (fresh or frozen)
4 tablespoons rice flour
1½ tablespoons water
300 g (10½ oz/2⅓ cups) sea salt

Stuff the cavity of the fish with the herb sprigs, lemongrass and makrut lime leaves. You want the cavity to be nicely stuffed, as these aromatics will flavour the fish as it cooks. Fasten the cavity closed using cocktail sticks (toothpicks).

Mix the rice flour and water together in a small bowl. The mixture should be slightly malleable but not overly wet, as you are going to rub this on the skin of the fish in order to create a 'glue' to help the salt adhere.

Lay the fish on a baking sheet, then rub the rice flour mix on to one side of the fish. I do this from tail to head, going against the direction of the fish scales. Ensure the whole side is covered in a thin white layer, then sprinkle generously with the sea salt to cover. Gently pat the salt on to the skin of the fish to ensure it adheres. Leave this side of the fish for 5 minutes so the salt dries slightly and sticks firmly to the fish.

Flip the fish over and repeat the process to cover the second side with salt. Don't be afraid to use a lot of salt when doing this; you want to create a thick salt crust or shell to protect the fish while cooking.

Prepare a charcoal grill and cook the fish over a consistent medium heat for 8 minutes on each side: the salt should become golden, slightly charred and rock hard before you turn it. To check if the fish is done, insert the tip of a sharp knife or a metal skewer into the thickest section behind the fish's head by the central spine. If the juices run clear and the tip of the knife is warm, the fish will be cooked. Leave to rest for a few minutes before peeling back the salt-crusted skin to reveal the cooked flesh. It's worth noting you will want to discard the skin unless you have a love of incredibly salty things! My preference is to serve the salt-crusted fish with a pile of lettuce leaves, herb sprigs and coiled rice noodles so that you can eat the fish in DIY lettuce-cup form. Then drizzle over the spicy seafood sauce (*nahm jim talay*) from page 74.

nahm prik / lon

Relishes

Relishes and dips, in particular *nahm prik*, are some of the most ancient dishes in the Thai culinary repertoire, as the ingredients used and the techniques employed date back to the earliest recordings of Thai cookery. The very earliest *nahm prik* would have involved peppercorns for spice, fermented soybeans for salty depth, and garlic and shallots for richness. Sour leaves and fruits like tamarind would have been used before the appearance of the now abundant lime, while sweetening agents like sugar wouldn't have featured until much later. Nowadays, these principal flavours are still upheld, but the building blocks have shifted to include some of Thailand's expanded and adopted ingredients, including fresh chillies, shrimp paste and sugar. The very nature of *nahm prik* is to provide flavour to accompanying dishes, such as rice, and they are aggressive in their seasoning by Western terms. Most, if not all, *nahm prik* relishes have pungent ingredients at their core that are either fermented, salted or pickled, and these ensure that flavours are bold and unforgettable.

Lon are not as ancient as *nahm prik* as they include coconut cream, an ingredient discovered by the Thai people as they spread southwards from their northern homelands during the 13th century. Essentially, the pungent *nahm prik* ingredients are simmered in fresh coconut cream, tempering their aggressive flavours and mellowing them, producing an unctuously rich sauce for dipping other ingredients into. *Lon* relishes include more sugar and have proteins such as minced (ground) prawns (shrimp), fatty pork and crab folded through them for body and decadence, with the addition of chopped red shallots, sour fruits and herbs contrasting with the otherwise silky texture.

nahm prik pao

Roasted Chilli Jam

This highly complex and luxuriously rich relish (*nahm prik*) can be used as far more than just a chilli dip. It can be thinned and the seasoning adjusted for salad dressings, or it can be made into a umami-rich stir-fry sauce that's especially good with shellfish. It's the Thai equivalent of the famous XO sauce used in Chinese cuisine. At the restaurant, we take influence from these traditional XO sauces by curing, smoking and drying scallop roes before deep-frying and adding them to the chilli jam (*nahm prik pao*) alongside dried shrimp. It's quite a time-consuming process, although I feel the resulting chilli paste is worth the labour. This recipe will make a fairly large quantity, about 2 litres (68 fl oz/8 cups), but the end result lasts indefinitely and is useful to have around at all times.

SERVES 8

1 teaspoon shrimp paste
banana leaf (optional)
vegetable oil, for deep-frying
70 g (2½ oz/1 cup) dried prawns
   (shrimp)
87 g (3 oz/1 cup) dried long red
   chillies, seeded and stems removed
75 g (2½ oz) galangal, thinly sliced
340 g (12 oz/4 cups) Fried Shallots
   (*hom jiaw*) (page 210)
270 g (10 oz/2 cups) Fried Garlic
   (*gratiam jiaw*) (page 211)
170 g (6 oz/1 cup) palm sugar
120 ml (4 fl oz/½ cup) Tamarind
   Water (*nahm makham piak*)
   (see page 214)
3 tablespoons fish sauce

Wrap the shrimp paste in the banana leaf or some kitchen foil and dry-toast in a pan over a low heat for 2 minutes, or until fragrant, flipping once during cooking. Set aside.

Pour the oil for deep-frying into a large wok to a depth of 5 cm (2 in). Heat to 180°C (350°F) on a cooking thermometer. Alternatively, drop a small cube of bread into the hot oil; if it turns golden brown in about 15 seconds, the oil is ready. Deep-fry the dried prawns, red chillies and galangal separately in the hot oil until golden and fragrant. Remove and drain on a plate lined with paper towels.

Transfer the toasted shrimp paste to a food processor, along with the deep-fried prawns, chillies and galangal, as well as the Fried Shallots and Fried Garlic. Blend to a smooth paste, using some of the frying oil (about 225 ml/8 fl oz/1 cup) to help emulsify the ingredients together.

Add the mixture to a saucepan over a low heat and bring to a simmer. Add the sugar, Tamarind Water and fish sauce and simmer gently for 5 minutes until thickened and jammy. Be careful not to simmer for too long, as the caramelising sugars will seize as it cools, making the jam impossible to use in the future. It will taste sweet, rich and spicy, with a little background tartness and saltiness.

Transfer to a container and top with more of the reserved frying oil to cover the surface of the chilli jam. Leave to cool before storing indefinitely in an airtight container in the refrigerator.

SERVE WITH

- Vegetables (*pak*) (page 88–89)
- Deep-fried Vegetables (*pak tort*) (page 89)
- Thai Omelette (*kai jiaw*) (page 90)
- Ayutthaya Grilled Native Lobster (*goong yai pao*) (page 74)

nahm prik num

Grilled Long Chilli Relish

This *nahm prik* from Northern Thailand is the one that sold me on their addictive moreishness. Don't be put off by the description: yes, this relish is made from grilled chillies, but that doesn't mean it's overly hot or spicy. In fact, most versions I've tried are well rounded and have a lovely depth of flavour from the charcoal grilling process, which imparts a subtle smokiness to the finished dip. In keeping with the region, fermented fish sauce (*nahm pla raa*) or in some cases fermented black crab paste (*nahm bpu*) is used to season the dip, but using regular fish sauce or salt works just as well.

SERVES 4

6 Turkish peppers (sivri biber chilli peppers) or 1 regular green (bell) pepper
4 long green chillies
1 large garlic bulb (80 g/3 oz), unpeeled
1 large banana shallot (100 g/3½ oz), unpeeled
3 green bird's eye chillies
1 tablespoon chopped coriander (cilantro) root or coriander stem
1 teaspoon salt
1 teaspoon caster (superfine) sugar
2 tablespoons fish sauce
1 teaspoon lime juice
1 tablespoon roughly chopped coriander (cilantro) sprigs
1 tablespoon thinly sliced sawtooth coriander (cilantro) or green tops of spring onions (scallions)

Soak 10 bamboo skewers in a large bowl of water for 1 hour, then thread the Turkish peppers, long green chillies, garlic cloves, shallot and bird's eye chillies on to them, using separate skewers for the different ingredients.

Prepare a charcoal grill. When the fire has died down and the coals are red-hot, cook the Turkish peppers and long green chillies for 5 minutes, until the skins are blackened and the insides are juicy. Leave to cool.

Once the coals are at a medium heat, cook the garlic, shallot and bird's eye chillies for 10 minutes. Again, you want to blacken and blister these ingredients, while ensuring the insides are cooked through, softened and tender to the touch. Leave to cool.

Peel the Turkish peppers and long chillies, but don't be too fastidious, as including some of the blackened skin in the finished dish will add to the smoky flavour. Discard the stems and seeds. Peel the garlic cloves and shallot and roughly chop. Don't worry about peeling or removing the seeds from the bird's eye chillies.

In a clay pestle and mortar, pound together the coriander root, salt and sugar. Add the grilled garlic and shallot and pound again to form a smooth paste. Add the bird's eye chillies and roughly pound these into a coarse paste. Remember, the finer these chillies become, the hotter the final dish will be. Finally, add the peeled Turkish peppers and long chillies. Try to pound these down the sides of the mortar and into long, thin strands as opposed to a smooth paste. The end result should be a slightly coarse and chunky dip.

When you have reached the desired texture, season the relish with the fish sauce and lime juice, then fold through the corianders. Serve in a small bowl.

SERVE WITH

- Chiang Mai Herbal Sausage (*sai ua*) (page 70)
- Pork Scratchings (*khaep mu*) (page 91)
- Thai Fried Chicken (*gai tort*) (page 116)
- Sticky Rice (*khao neow*) (page 196)

akhar sapi thong

Akhar Tribe Cashew and Dill Relish

I first got the idea for this recipe when travelling around Northern Thailand. I was fortunate enough to visit a number of local hill tribes, in particular the Akhar and Lahu people, learning first-hand about the indigenous ingredients and cooking methods of the region. I remember on one occasion being shown how to make a traditional roasted peanut relish called *akhar sapi thong* that was utterly delicious. I decided to make my own version using similar ingredients and herbs that mirrored the flavours of the wild shoots and leaves that the Akhar people forage and use in their cooking.

SERVES 4

200 g (7 oz/1¼ cups) raw cashew nuts, or another nut of your choice
6 cherry tomatoes (use slightly unripe tomatoes so they have a tartness)
2 tablespoons water
2 bird's eye chillies, chopped
1 tablespoon chopped coriander (cilantro) root or coriander stem
1 tablespoon chopped garlic
1 teaspoon salt
1 teaspoon palm or brown sugar
1 tablespoon yellow soybean sauce
2 tablespoons finely chopped tender dill tips, plus 3 extra dill tips, to garnish
2 tablespoons finely chopped coriander sprigs
1 tablespoon finely chopped marjoram leaves
1 bunch radishes (preferably with leafy tops), halved, to serve

Preheat the oven to 180°C (350°F/gas 4). Spread out the cashews on a baking tray (pan) and toast in the oven for 10 minutes, stirring frequently, until golden brown and smelling roasted and nutty. Leave to cool.

Warm the cherry tomatoes and water in a small saucepan over a medium heat for 2 minutes until the tomatoes begin to roast and blister. Stir the tomatoes around the pan until the water is reduced and evaporated and the tomatoes soft, blistered and collapsed.

In a pestle and mortar, pound together the chillies, coriander root, garlic, salt and sugar to form a smooth paste. Still pounding, gradually add three-quarters of the roasted cashews, mixing and stirring as you go, as they can become stiff in the mortar. Pound the final one-quarter of the cashews coarsely into the paste to leave some texture.

Add the soybean sauce and blistered tomatoes to the cashew paste and mix together while gently crushing the tomatoes. The juice from the tomatoes will loosen the paste and give it the viscosity of a very thick peanut butter.

Fold the chopped herbs through the cashew paste and taste; it should be roasted and nutty, well-seasoned with a background spice and herbal flavour. If required, add more soybean sauce and/or salt as necessary. Transfer to a small bowl, garnish with the dill tips and serve with the radishes for dipping.

lon gapi

Fragrant Shrimp and Coconut Cream Relish

This is a delicious relish that shares similarities with the widely known coconut cream curries of Thailand. There is some overlap in the fundamental ingredients used and the cooking style. The process involves frying a fragrant paste that resonates in fermented shrimp paste (*gapi*) with rich coconut cream; resulting in a luscious and moreish dip for raw vegetables and sour fruits. This dip is also wonderful with freshly fried prawn crackers which are available in Asian supermarkets (grocery stores), sold as thin round discs that require frying in hot vegetable oil.

SERVES 4

250 ml (9 fl oz/1 cup plus
  1 tablespoon) coconut cream (the
  richer, heavier solids that rise to the
  top of the thinner milk)
1 tablespoon coconut oil
3 tablespoons palm or brown sugar
2 tablespoons Tamarind Water (*nahm
  makham piak*) (page 214)
1 tablespoon fish sauce
150 ml (5 fl oz/⅔ cup) coconut milk
juice of 1 mandarin or clementine
½ small red onion, cut into 5 mm
  (¼ in) slices with the grain of the
  onion
1 long red chilli, thickly sliced into
  5 mm (¼ in) rounds
1 tablespoon fingerroot, thinly sliced
  on the diagonal (optional)
1 tablespoon coriander (cilantro)
  leaves

For the relish paste (*khreuang lon*)

4 tablespoons dried shrimp
5 dried long red chillies, seeded and
  soaked in cold water for 15 minutes
  until soft
1 teaspoon salt
3 tablespoons thinly sliced
  lemongrass, root and outer
  husks removed
1 tablespoon chopped galangal
2 tablespoons chopped banana
  shallot
3 tablespoons chopped garlic
1 teaspoon chopped turmeric root or
  ½ tablespoon ground turmeric
3 tablespoons chopped fingerroot,
  (this is a key ingredient, but if
  impossible to source then substitute
  with 2 tablespoons chopped
  ginger root)
4 tablespoons shrimp paste

For the relish paste, pound all the ingredients together in a stone pestle and mortar until very smooth (see pages 204–207 for an expanded explanation on efficiently pounding a paste).

Heat the coconut cream and oil together in a saucepan over a medium heat to separate and 'crack' the cream (see page 209 on separating coconut cream). Add the paste to the separated cream, stir and fry over a medium–low heat for 10 minutes until fragrant. Season with the sugar, Tamarind Water and fish sauce, then stir in the coconut milk and simmer for a few more minutes until the mixture darkens in colour and has an oily sheen.

Remove from the heat and season with the mandarin juice. Stir through the sliced onion and chilli, along with most of the sliced fingerroot. The relish should taste rich, pungent and salty from the shrimp paste and dried shrimp, with background earthy tones from the fingerroot and a fruity tartness from the tamarind. Transfer to a small dish, then top with the remaining sliced fingerroot and the coriander leaves and serve.

SERVE WITH

- Vegetables (*pak*) (pages 88–89)
- Ayutthaya Grilled Native Lobster (*goong yai pao*) (page 74)
- Thai Omelette (*kai jiaw*) (page 90)
- Fish Cakes with Cucumber Pickle (*tort man pla*) (page 120)

kreaung kiam

Accompaniments

Nahm prik relishes are not designed to be eaten on their own, and are always accompanied with side dishes. These side dishes range from the very simple, such as a plate of raw vegetable crudités, to more elaborate offerings that feel like a dish in their own right, such as Sweet Candied Pork (*mu waan*). This section contains recipes for a select few accompaniments, but by no means is this list exhaustive.

pak
Vegetables

These are the most common accompaniments to *nahm prik* and it would be rare not to have some variety of vegetables and herbs to be eaten alongside. The vegetables can either be served raw, boiled, steamed, barbecued (grilled), pickled or deep-fried, with each preparation offering different flavour dimensions and textures. The list of vegetables and herbs you can partner is endless, so just go wild and use your imagination, guided by seasonality and freshness. I've given some examples of my favourite vegetables and herbs to use, and some guidance on how they should be cut to create a natural vessel to dip into the various *nahm prik* relishes.

Raw

- White cabbage, cut into wedges
- Cucumber, cut into bite-size lengths
- Radishes, whole or halved, preferably with leafy tops
- Iceberg lettuce, cut into wedges or leaves separated
- Green tomatoes, quartered
- Fine green beans, trimmed
- Fennel, cut into bite-size pieces
- Cape gooseberries or physalis
- Granny Smith apples, or any other sharp apple variety, cut into wedges
- Grapefruit, segmented, with thick membrane removed
- Bitter leaves, such as chicory, endive and radicchio, leaves separated
- Herb sprigs, such as coriander (cilantro), dill, chervil, hot mint and Thai basil
- Herb leaves, such as nasturtium, garden sorrel, sawtooth coriander (cilantro), wild pepper and perilla

Boiled or steamed

- Pumpkin or squash, seeded and cut into wedges
- Asparagus spears
- Sweetheart cabbage, cut into wedges
- Fine green beans, trimmed
- Purple/white sprouting broccoli

Grilled

- Mushrooms, such as oyster, king oyster, shimeji, girolles or wild ceps, brushed with a little oil or fat
- Bitter leaves, such as chicory, endive and radicchio, halved or quartered, brushed with a little oil
- Asparagus spears, brushed with a little oil
- Aubergine (eggplant), cut into slices and brushed with a little oil
- Celeriac (celery root), thickly sliced, brushed with a little coconut cream

pak tort
Deep-fried vegetables

Deep-fried vegetables hold the same principle as Japanese tempura where vegetables are coated in a wet batter before deep-frying in plenty of oil. The best vegetables for this method are those that cook quickly. In Thailand many cooks use a shop-bought tempura mix. If you see this in your Asian supermarket (grocery store) then do feel free to use it. Otherwise, I've included a recipe for a coconut cream batter which I use with the vegetables listed below.

- Mushrooms, such as oyster, king oyster, shimeji, enoki and shiitake
- Fine green beans, trimmed
- Purple/white sprouting broccoli
- Pumpkin or squash, seeded and cut into 1 cm (½ in) slices
- Asparagus spears
- Wild garlic leaves
- Wild pepper leaves
- Herb sprigs, such as coriander (cilantro), chervil and Thai basil

For the coconut cream batter
150 g (5 oz/scant 1 cup) rice flour
50 g (2 oz/½ cup) tapioca flour
1 tablespoon salt
2 tablespoons coconut cream
350 ml (12 fl oz/¾ cup) chilled sparkling water
vegetable oil, for deep-frying
fine salt

Combine the flours and salt in a wide bowl. Add the coconut cream and whisk to create a very thick batter. Continue to whisk as you gradually add the sparkling water to create a thinner batter. Pour the oil into a large wok to a depth of 10 cm (4 in) and heat until the oil reaches 180°C (350°F) on a cooking thermometer. Alternatively, drop in a small cube of bread; if it turns golden brown in about 15 seconds, the oil is ready. Dip the prepared vegetables into the batter, then deep-fry for 1 minute, until golden brown and crispy. Drain on paper towels and season with fine salt before serving.

pak dong
Pickled Vegetables

Traditionally, pickled vegetables are eaten with relishes that are hot and salty, with little sourness or sweetness, as the sweet pickle liquor used provides these flavour traits. Below are some of my favourite vegetables to use with the pickle liquid recipe given.

- Baby onions or shallots, peeled and halved/quartered depending on their size
- Radishes, halved/quartered depending on their size
- Baby cucumbers, whole or halved
- Fine green beans, trimmed
- Carrots, sliced or shredded
- White part of the watermelon rind, skin peeled, cut into bite-size pieces and soaked overnight in slightly salted water
- Whole bird's eye chillies
- Long red/green chillies, sliced
- Three-cornered leeks, cut into 3 cm (1¼ in) lengths
- Wild garlic leaves

For the pickle liquid (*nahm dong*)
200 ml (7 fl oz/scant 1 cup) white vinegar (or rice vinegar)
200 ml (7 fl oz/scant 1 cup) water
2 tablespoons salt
140 g (5 oz/⅔ cup) caster (superfine) sugar
1 pandan leaf, knotted (optional)
1 dried mandarin peel (page 34), optional

For the pickle liquid, bring the vinegar, water, salt and sugar to the boil in a large saucepan. Reduce the heat to a simmer and cook for 3 minutes, or until the sugar has completely dissolved. Remove from heat and add the knotted pandan leaf and dried mandarin peel, if using. Leave to cool completely before immersing the vegetables of your choice for at least 1 hour. Serve.

kai jiaw
Thai Omelette

Eggs are widely eaten in Thailand, and a personal favourite is this simple omelette, which benefits from shallow-frying in smoking oil (or pork fat) so the edges become crispy while the centre remains soft. This omelette can be enjoyed with freshly steamed rice, some sliced raw cucumber and a bowl of Thai sriracha sauce for a simple light meal. Omit the dried shrimp if making a vegetarian version.

3 large eggs
½ teaspoon salt
¼ teaspoon ground white pepper
1 tablespoon dried shrimp, soaked in warm water for 5 minutes until tender, then drained
6 tablespoons vegetable oil or rendered pork fat (page 216)

Whisk the eggs, salt, white pepper and dried shrimp together in a large bowl until the eggs are well beaten. Heat the oil or fat in a large wok over a high heat until very hot, almost at smoking point. Carefully pour the eggs directly into the hot oil. The eggs will splutter, puffing up like a soufflé. Fry for 1 minute until the omelette develops a crispy bottom, flipping once to set on the other side. Drain on a plate lined with paper towels before serving.

khaep mu
Pork Scratchings

A speciality of Northern Thailand, particularly around Chiang Mai, where people eat pork scratchings with Grilled Long Chilli Relish (*nahm prik num*) (page 83) and several other dishes. That's not to say pork scratchings aren't enjoyed in other regions of Thailand; in fact, because of their popularity, many different recipes exist for these addictive puffed pork scratchings.

2 tablespoons white wine vinegar
1 tablespoon salt, plus extra to serve
200 g (7 oz) pork skin, excess fat removed
vegetable oil, for deep-frying

Bring a large saucepan of water to the boil with the vinegar and salt. Add the pork skin and gently boil for 50–60 minutes until it is tender and slightly translucent. Remove from the pan and leave to cool, before scraping away any excess fat. Cut the pork skin into rectangular pieces, each about 5 × 2 cm (2 × ¾ in), then place on a wire rack and dry out in a low oven or dehydrator set at 50°C (122°F) until completely dry. The skin will keep like this for up to a month in an airtight container in the refrigerator.

Pour the oil for deep-frying into a large wok to a depth of 10 cm (4 in) and heat until the oil reaches 200°C (400°F) on a cooking thermometer. Alternatively, drop a small cube of bread into the hot oil; if it turns golden brown in about 10 seconds, the oil is ready. Deep-fry the dried skin in small batches until the skin puffs and expands. Drain on a plate lined with paper towels and season with fine salt before serving.

mu waan
Sweet Candied Pork

Sweet pork is served with a number of different *nahm prik* relishes as a sticky-sweet accompaniment, or it can simply be eaten as a side dish to a wider meal.

3 tablespoons light soy sauce
1 tablespoon caster (superfine) sugar
350 g (12 oz) pork belly, shoulder or neck
5 tablespoons palm sugar
3 tablespoons fish sauce
2 tablespoons water
1 star anise, toasted
2.5 cm (1 in) piece of cassia bark, toasted
1 pandan leaf, knotted
red onion, sliced
coriander (cilantro), chopped

In a bowl, combine the soy sauce and caster sugar, then massage this mixture all over the pork. Transfer to a sealed container and leave to marinate overnight in the refrigerator.

The next day, steam the pork in a bamboo steamer set over a pan of water over a high heat for 30 minutes, or until tender. Leave to cool, then slice the pork into bite-size pieces, each about 3 × 1 cm (1¼ × ½ in).

Melt the palm sugar in a wok or saucepan over a low heat until liquid, then simmer for 2 minutes to darken and caramelise. Add the fish sauce and water, then add the sliced pork, star anise, cassia bark and pandan leaf and mix everything together so the pork is well coated in the caramel. Simmer gently for 10 minutes, or until slightly reduced and the pork is shiny. Take off the heat and leave the pork to rest in the caramel for 15 minutes before warming through and serving sprinkled with sliced red onion and chopped coriander.

SERVE WITH
• Fried Shallots (*hom jiaw*) (page 210)

dtom

Soups and Braises

In Thai culture, soups are viewed in a different light to those eaten in Western cuisine. They are eaten in conjunction with a meal to restore the palate from other more aggressive dishes laced with chillies and pungent seasonings. At their most basic, a simple stock or bone broth is simmered with a few aromatics and lightly seasoned. This style of broth is known as *gaeng jeut* and has the unfortunate translation of 'bland liquid', which I find unflattering and unjust. Instead, I refer to them as 'simple soups' that show restraint and bring balance to a wider meal with their subtle seasonings and comforting flavour profiles. In keeping with the evolution of Thai cuisine, today's soups find themselves with more elaborate ingredients and complex seasonings. This is seen most famously in *dtom yum*, the world-renowned hot and sour soup, and *dtom kha*, a rich and silky galangal and coconut cream soup.

Braising is a popular technique employed in Thai cuisine and one that I am particularly fond of, as it relies on time doing the heavy work for the cook, allowing tough cuts of meat to become succulently soft and yielding while melding with the flavours of the ingredients they are braised with. On the whole, Thai braises have a delicate and comforting nature to them, designed to be eaten with plenty of soothing rice and in the cooler months of the year. Braises revolve around a stock simmered with a protein, aromatics and vegetables, resulting in a flavour-packed broth that envelops the other ingredients, not dissimilar to a Thai soup.

dtom yum goong

Langoustine and Rhubarb Hot and Sour Soup

This is my version of the widely known hot and sour soup of Thailand. The word *dtom* translates to 'boil' and *yum* to 'mix' – in essence, a mixed boil of ingredients. At its heart, stock is perfumed with bruised aromatics such as lemongrass, galangal and makrut lime leaves, then seasoned with fresh chillies, fish sauce and lime juice, resulting in a soup that is hot, salty and sour. I like to showcase tart ingredients found in the British larder to replicate the bright sourness brought by lime juice. In this recipe, I have chosen forced rhubarb for its attractive pink colour and vibrant sour flavour.

SERVES 4

12 live langoustines
1 litre (34 fl oz/4 cups) Fish Stock (*nahm cheua pla*) (page 203)
5 cm (2 in) piece of galangal, peeled
2 lemongrass stalks, cut into 5 cm (2 in) batons
6 bird's eye chillies (fewer if you wish, but this soup should be spicy), plus 1 tablespoon, bruised, to garnish (optional)
4 makrut lime leaves (fresh or frozen), torn
4 tablespoons fish sauce
1 teaspoon caster (superfine) sugar
15 cm (6 in) forced Yorkshire rhubarb stalk, thinly sliced across the length
90 ml (3¼ fl oz/6 tablespoons) rhubarb juice from forced Yorkshire rhubarb
2 tablespoons lime juice
1 tablespoon coriander (cilantro) leaves
1 tablespoon Roasted Chilli Jam (*nahm prik pao*) (page 82), optional, to serve
salt

Freeze the langoustines for 15 minutes to stun them. Bring a large saucepan of water to the boil and season with 1 tablespoon of salt for every 1 litre (34 fl oz/4 cups) of water. Prepare a bowl of iced water. This is to stop the langoustines from cooking further after blanching. Add the langoustines to the boiling water and boil for 30 seconds before transferring them to the iced water. Do this in batches if necessary so as to not overcrowd the pan.

Prepare the langoustines by separating the heads from the bodies. The bodies have six hard joints; using your thumb and index finger, pinch the middle (third) joint to break the body shell. Now, holding the tail, you should be able to pull away the tail and last three shell joints from the body meat. If done correctly, you will also pull away the digestive tract. Now push and release the body meat from the top three joints of the shell, leaving you with the intact body meat. Repeat the process with all the langoustines. Should you need to remove the digestive tract from the body separately, use the tip of a sharp knife.

Place the langoustine heads, claws and shells into a wide-based saucepan and crush them using a pestle to break the heads and claws. Cover with the stock. Bring to the boil, then reduce the heat and simmer for 20 minutes until the stock develops a red hue from the tomalley in the langoustine heads. Strain through a sieve (fine-mesh strainer), pressing the heads, claws and shells to extract as much flavour as possible, then return the stock to the heat and bring back to the boil.

Bruise the galangal, lemongrass batons and chillies in a pestle and mortar, then add to the stock, along with the torn makrut lime leaves, fish sauce and sugar. Simmer for 1 minute before adding the par-cooked langoustine bodies and the sliced rhubarb, then simmer gently for 30 seconds until the langoustines are just cooked and the rhubarb has a slight bite.

Remove from the heat and season with the rhubarb and lime juices. It's important not to boil these juices, as they will become muted, dull and bitter, instead of remaining sharp and vibrant. The stock should taste spicy, salty and sour; adjust the seasoning as necessary to achieve this balance. Ladle the soup into serving bowls and garnish with coriander leaves and bruised bird's eye chillies. Finish by drizzling over the Roasted Chilli Jam, if using, and serve.

dtom kha hed ba

Coconut and Galangal Soup of Wild Mushrooms

This popular soup combines soothing coconut cream with aromatic and peppery galangal. It's not a spicy dish; instead, it's rich and comforting. Chicken is commonly braised into the soup throughout Thailand, but here I've opted to use a mix of cultivated and wild mushrooms. I use chicken stock in the recipe to give the soup body and depth, but using vegetable stock would be fine if you wanted to keep it vegetarian or vegan. Normally the galangal and lemongrass are bruised and infused into the soup, in the same fashion as the traditional hot and sour soup (*dtom yum*). However, my grandmother's version involves pounding these aromatics into a paste that is then dissolved into the soup, and that's what I've done here. This provides a richer flavour and makes the ingredients digestible.

SERVES 2

100 g (3½ oz) mixed mushrooms, such as oyster, shimeji, enoki and shiitake

50 g/2 oz wild mushrooms, such as girolles, trompette, chanterelles and hen of the woods

300 ml (10 fl oz/1¼ cups) coconut cream

200 ml (7 fl oz/scant 1 cup) Chicken Stock (*nahm cheua gai*) (page 200) or use Vegetable Stock (*nahm cheua jay*) (page 199) for a vegetarian/vegan version

1 tablespoon palm or caster (superfine) sugar

2 tablespoons thinly sliced galangal

4 makrut lime leaves (fresh or frozen), torn

3 bird's eye chillies, bruised

3 tablespoons fish sauce, or use light soy sauce for a vegetarian/vegan version

3 tablespoons lime juice

1 tablespoon roughly chopped coriander (cilantro) sprigs, to garnish

1 tablespoon Roasted Chilli Jam (*nahm prik pao*) (page 82), optional, to serve

For the paste

3 tablespoons chopped galangal

2 tablespoons thinly sliced lemongrass, root and outer husks removed

1 tablespoon chopped coriander (cilantro) root or coriander stem

2 tablespoons chopped round shallot

1 tablespoon chopped garlic

1 teaspoon salt

½ teaspoon white peppercorns

In a pestle and mortar, pound the galangal, lemongrass, coriander root, shallot, garlic, salt and white peppercorns to form a smooth paste.

Clean the mushrooms using a pastry brush to remove any dirt and grit. Do not wash them, as they will absorb the water and it will dilute their flavour. Tear or slice any larger mushrooms into bite-size pieces. Set aside.

Bring the coconut cream and stock to the boil in a large saucepan. Reduce the heat to a simmer, then add the sugar and pounded paste and simmer for 2 minutes, or until completely dissolved.

Add the galangal slices, torn makrut lime leaves, bruised chillies and mushrooms and simmer for 3 minutes, or until the mushrooms are cooked and the coconut cream has separated slightly.

Season with the fish sauce and taste. At this stage, the soup should taste rich and well-seasoned with a background warmth of chilli. Remove from the heat and finish the seasoning with lime juice; this will help cut through the richness of the coconut cream. Ladle the soup into serving bowls, garnish with the chopped coriander and drizzle each serving with the Roasted Chilli Jam, if using.

dtom kamin gai baan
Turmeric and Partridge Soup

This soup originates from Southern Thailand, where fresh turmeric is used plentifully in dishes, giving a distinctive medicinal earthiness and fragrance. It is common for Thai people to keep chickens at home for their eggs and meat. Due to the chickens' freely roaming lifestyle, they develop tougher but more flavourful, almost gamey meat. I'm a big fan of the poultry game we have available throughout the British Isles, and have opted to use partridge for this dish as it shares similarities with the chicken found in Thailand. Other poultry, such as pheasant, guinea fowl and chicken, would all work well in this recipe, but not those fattier birds with darker meat, such as duck, grouse and pigeon, whose flavours are too strong and overpowering against the delicate broth.

SERVES 4

2 whole partridges, ideally with offal (variety meats), about 275 g (10 oz) each
60 g (2 oz) chicken livers (optional)
1 litre (34 fl oz/4 cups) Chicken Stock (*nahm cheua gai*) (page 200)
3 tablespoons sliced galangal
3 lemongrass stalks, cut into 7.5 cm (3 in) batons and bruised
2 tablespoons turmeric root, peeled and bruised, or 1 tablespoon ground turmeric
1 small white onion, quartered
1 pandan leaf, knotted
1 teaspoon salt
½ teaspoon palm or caster (superfine) sugar
4 bird's eye chillies, bruised
4 makrut lime leaves (fresh or frozen), torn
3 tablespoons fish sauce
2 tablespoons Tamarind Water (*nahm makham piak*) (page 214)
1 tablespoon coriander (cilantro) leaves, to garnish

Prepare the partridges by removing the legs and separating the crown from the back section of the birds. Break the legs, back section and crown into bite-size pieces, keeping the flesh on the bone and keeping the skin on. Set the crown pieces aside for later. If using, prepare the partridge offal and chicken livers by trimming any sinew and slicing into elegant pieces of liver and heart.

Bring the stock to the boil in a large saucepan. Add the sliced galangal, bruised lemongrass, turmeric, onion, pandan leaf, salt and sugar, then reduce the heat to a simmer and add the chopped partridge legs and back section. Simmer for 30 minutes, or until the meat is tender and pulling away from the bone, but still has a slight bounce.

Remove the pandan leaf and discard. Bring the stock back to the boil, then add the bruised chillies, makrut lime leaves, fish sauce and Tamarind Water. Simmer for a few more minutes to allow the flavours to infuse. At this stage, the soup should taste earthy from the turmeric and fragrant from the lemongrass, with a gentle background warmth of chilli. It should be well-seasoned, with a fruity-tart sweetness from the tamarind.

Add the pieces of crown/breast meat and simmer for another 2 minutes, or until just cooked. Drop in the thinly sliced liver and heart, if using, then ladle into serving bowls and garnish with coriander leaves to serve.

gaeng jeut

Shiitake Mushroom and Thai Basil Soup with Tapioca Pearls

Tapioca pearls are used in Thailand to give texture and body to *gaeng jeut*-style 'simple soups' with their thickening starch properties. Although out of favour with many Westerners, I'm actually fond of the almost jelly-like and bouncy feel of the pearls when sipping on these soothing soups. My preference is to use the larger pearls, which take a little longer to cook but offer a superior texture compared with the smaller ones. This mellow soup uses chicken stock as the base, but vegetable stock would work fine if you wanted to keep it vegetarian or vegan-friendly. Some strands of torn roasted chicken or picked white crab meat would add an extra dimension to this soup, as would the addition of other mushrooms, such as oyster, shimeji or girolles. Use this as a base to experiment with other flavours and see what suits you.

SERVES 2

4 tablespoons tapioca pearls (large or small)

1 teaspoon salt

800 ml (28 fl oz/3½ cups) Chicken Stock (*nahm cheua gai*) (page 200) or Vegetable Stock (*nahm cheua jay*) (page 199)

1 tablespoon oyster sauce (omit if vegetarian/vegan and increase the light soy sauce)

2 tablespoons light soy sauce

¼ teaspoon ground white pepper

1 teaspoon palm or caster (superfine) sugar

8 fresh shiitake mushrooms, sliced, or use dried ones soaked in cold water for 2 hours until tender

2–3 tablespoons coconut water (not coconut milk or cream, but the translucent, sweet water)

2 spring onions (scallions), thinly sliced

4 tablespoons Thai basil leaves, plus extra for topping

1 teaspoon Fried Garlic and Fragrant Garlic Oil (*gratiam jiaw*) (page 211)

½ teaspoon sesame oil

Wash the tapioca pearls in a sieve under cold running water, then set aside. Bring plenty of water to the boil in a tall saucepan and add the salt. Using a whisk, constantly stir the boiling water while adding the tapioca pearls, then whisk for 1 minute to break up any clumps and prevent the pearls sticking to the base of the pan. Reduce the heat to low and simmer, stirring frequently with a whisk, for about 15–30 minutes until the pearls are tender and translucent. Drain and rinse the pearls under cold running water so they don't clump together.

Bring the stock to the boil in a large saucepan and season with the oyster sauce, soy sauce, pepper and sugar. Reduce the heat to low and simmer for 1 minute, then add the mushrooms and tapioca pearls. Heat the ingredients through gently for 1 minute, but do not boil the stock.

Remove the pan from the heat and stir through the coconut water, spring onions and Thai basil. Ladle into serving bowls and top with extra Thai basil leaves, then drizzle with the Fried Garlic and Fragrant Garlic Oil and the sesame oil. The soup should be well-seasoned with a slight nuttiness from the sesame oil.

mu hong

Phuket Town Black Pepper Pork

I first tried this dish in a restaurant specialising in Southern Thai cooking: Prai Raya, the Bangkok outpost of Raya, a Phuket Town dining institution. I'd eaten Southern food on many occasions but strangely had never come across *mu hong* until my cousin ordered it during a family gathering. The dish arrived as glistening chunks of pork belly, tender and wobbly but holding their shape, and coated in a dark caramelised gravy heavy with black pepper. The pork was unctuously soft and melting, with the perfect balance of fat to keep the meat moist and juicy. The taste was not overly sweet, but instead rich and savoury thanks to the black pepper and soy sauce. It was fantastic, and I've been making this version ever since. Using sugar as a preservation method is key to Thai cooking; with that in mind, consider making this dish a day or two before you intend to eat it so the flavours deepen and develop to dizzying heights.

SERVES 8

800 g (1 lb 12 oz) pork belly, cut into 4 cm (1½ in) cubes
3 tablespoons chopped coriander (cilantro) root or coriander stem
3 tablespoons chopped garlic
2 tablespoons black peppercorns
4 tablespoons rendered pork fat (page 216)
5 tablespoons palm or brown sugar
2 tablespoons black soy sauce
3 star anise, toasted
5 cm (2 in) piece of cassia bark, toasted
1 tablespoon white cardamom pods (about 6 pods), toasted
2 bay leaves (fresh or dried)
1 litre (34 fl oz/4 cups) Pork Stock (*nahm cheua mu*) (page 201)
3 tablespoons light soy sauce
1 dried mandarin peel (page 34), optional
1 pandan leaf, knotted (optional)
2 tablespoons coriander (cilantro) sprigs, snipped into shorter sprigs of leaf and stem
salt

SERVE WITH

- Steamed Jasmine Rice (*khao hom mali*) (pages 194–195)
- Pickled Vegetables (*pak dong*) (page 90)

Wash the pork belly under cold running water, then transfer to a large stockpot and cover with water that's been lightly seasoned with salt. Bring to the boil, then drain and wash the pork belly and stockpot of any scum. Repeat this cold-blanching process once more, then set the washed pork belly aside. This will remove impurities from the meat, giving you a clear final sauce and reducing the cooking time. If you prefer to skip this step, that's fine; as mentioned, the cook time will be longer and the final broth will be cloudy, but the finished dish will be equally delicious!

In a pestle and mortar, pound the coriander root, garlic, peppercorns and 1 teaspoon of salt to a coarse paste. Heat the pork fat in a wok or heavy-based saucepan over a medium heat. Add the paste and fry for 3–5 minutes until aromatic and fragrant, then add the blanched pork belly and begin to sear and lightly colour the meat all over, stirring all the while to prevent the meat from catching and burning.

Add the sugar, black soy sauce, star anise, cassia bark, cardamom pods and bay leaves. Allow the sugar to melt and caramelise with the pork belly; it should stick and cling to the meat. Stir to evenly coat all the meat with the caramel.

Add the stock, then season with the light soy sauce. Add the dried mandarin peel and knotted pandan leaf, if using. Bring to the boil, then reduce to a simmer and cook for 2–3 hours until the pork belly is tender but holds its shape with a slight bounce, topping up the pan with extra stock or water as required during the cooking time to keep the meat covered.

Increase the heat and cook for another 10–15 minutes to reduce the braising liquor by half so that it's thick and glossy and coats the meat. Be sure to stir the meat during this step so that it doesn't catch and burn on the base of the pan. The desired consistency should coat the back of a spoon, and it should taste sweet and savoury with a peppery finish. Top with snipped coriander sprigs and serve.

bpet parlow

Five-spice Duck with Soy-stained Duck Eggs

The original Chinese origins of *parlow* are clearly tasted via the familiar underlying flavour of Chinese five-spice powder. Huge bubbling woks of *parlow* are a common sight in almost any market in Thailand. This dish is most commonly made using pork, but I find duck and even goose work very well with the fragrant dried spices. In this recipe, I marinate the duck in black soy sauce and deep-fry it to seal the meat while giving it an attractive golden-brown colour. If you prefer to omit this step, then it won't overly detract from the flavour, and will make the recipe less arduous. I have included a recipe for my own spice blend powder, but using shop-bought five-spice will work perfectly well and is commonplace with cooks in Thailand.

SERVES 6

4 duck eggs
1 tablespoon black soy sauce, plus
　4 tablespoons extra for marinating
　the duck eggs and duck meat
1 whole duck, about 1.5–2 kg (3 lb
　5 oz–4 lb 8 oz); Gressingham and
　Aylesbury are both fine breeds
vegetable oil, for deep-frying
2 tablespoons chopped coriander
　(cilantro) root or coriander stem
2 tablespoons chopped ginger
4 tablespoons chopped garlic
½ tablespoon white peppercorns
½ tablespoon salt
2 tablespoons vegetable oil (if you
　don't want to render the duck fat)
2 white cardamom pods
1 star anise
5 cm (2 in) piece of cassia bark
3 tablespoons palm or brown sugar
2 tablespoons fish sauce
1 tablespoon light soy sauce
1 tablespoon oyster sauce
2 litres (68 fl oz/8 cups) Chicken
　Stock (*nahm cheua gai*) (page 200)
1 dried mandarin peel
1 pandan leaf, knotted
10 dried shiitake mushrooms, tough
　stems removed
2 tablespoons roughly chopped
　coriander (cilantro) sprigs

For the spice blend, pound all the ingredients together in a pestle and mortar, or grind in a spice grinder or small food processer to a powder, then set aside. The spice blend will keep for up to a month in an airtight container placed in the refrigerator.

Have a bowl of iced water ready nearby. Bring a medium saucepan of water to the boil, then add the duck eggs and boil for 6 minutes for soft-boiled or 10 minutes for hard-boiled. Plunge into the bowl of iced water to stop them cooking further, then peel and coat in 2 tablespoons of the black soy sauce. Transfer to a container and leave to marinate in the refrigerator.

Meanwhile, break down the duck by removing the legs and wings, then separating the crown from the back section. Using a cleaver or heavy knife, chop the legs, wings and back section into bite-size pieces, with the meat still attached to the bone. Cut the crown into two breast sections, then cut the breast into bite-size pieces, still attached to the crown bone. Mix the duck pieces with 2 tablespoons of the black soy sauce and leave to marinate for 1 hour in the refrigerator.

You will be left with excess duck fat and skin from breaking down the bird. Mince (grind) any duck skin, then transfer the fat and skin to a saucepan with 1 tablespoon of water. Warm over a low heat for 10 minutes, or until the fat is rendered and the moisture has evaporated, then pass through a strainer (fine-mesh sieve) into a bowl. The crispy skin can be kept to garnish this dish or it can be added to salads or *laab* for texture. Set the duck fat aside for later.

Pour the oil for deep-frying into a wok or tall saucepan to a depth of about 8 cm (3¼ in) and heat until it has reached 160°C (325°F) on a cooking thermometer. Alternatively, drop a small cube of bread into the hot oil; if it turns golden brown in about 30 seconds, the oil is ready. Drain the duck of any excess

For the spice blend powder
(*pong parlow*)

4 × 10 cm (2 × 4 in) piece of
  cassia bark
3 tablespoons star anise
2 tablespoons coriander seeds
1 tablespoon fennel seeds
1 tablespoon cloves
1 teaspoon Sichuan peppercorns

marinade, then deep-fry, in batches, for 3 minutes, or until dark golden. Remove and leave to drain on paper towels.

In a pestle and mortar, pound the coriander root, ginger, garlic, peppercorns and salt to a coarse paste. Heat the rendered duck fat (or vegetable oil, if you skipped that step) in a wok or large saucepan over a medium heat, then add the paste and fry until aromatic and golden brown. Add the cardamom pods, star anise, cassia bark and 1 tablespoon of the spice blend powder and fry for another minute until fragrant.

Add the sugar, fish sauce, light soy sauce, oyster sauce and black soy sauce and heat until the sugar is completely dissolved and begins to caramelise, then moisten with the stock. Add the dried mandarin peel, pandan leaf, shiitake mushrooms and deep-fried duck pieces. Bring to the boil, then reduce to a simmer and braise for 2 hours, or until the duck meat is tender and the liquor has reduced by one-third. The duck will release plenty of fat during this cooking time, which should be skimmed off and kept for another use.

Meanwhile, remove about 200 ml (7 fl oz/scant 1 cup) of the braising liquor and pour it over the marinated duck eggs until they are submerged. Leave at room temperature to stain the eggs, or overnight if you plan to reheat and eat the dish the next day.

When the duck is fully braised and tender, check the seasoning. It should be well-seasoned, with the rich and warming flavour of the dried spices. When ready to serve, add the marinated duck eggs and their liquor to the pan and warm through gently. Serve in a large dish, sprinkled with chopped coriander. You can choose to discard the bony wings and backbone sections, but Thai people will happily gnaw on these parts of the duck, and you may wish to also!

SERVE WITH
- Pickled Vegetables (*pak dong*) (page 90)
- Steamed Jasmine Rice (*khao hom mali*) (page 194–195)

Five-spice Duck with Soy-stained Duck Eggs

tort / pad

Fried /Stir-fried

Fried and deep-fried foods are popular in modern-day Thailand, but this wasn't always the case, as historically the technique requires copious amounts of rendered pork fat or coconut oil, which were expensive and not plentiful. As such, these traditional cooking fats were considered luxury items and therefore so was the technique of deep-frying. Nowadays, cooks have abundant access to inexpensive vegetable oils, and the sight of woks filled with bubbling oil is commonplace across the markets and street corners of Thailand. Similar to Western cooking methods, items are dusted or battered, then briefly immersed in hot oil over a high heat until just cooked. However, in some instances, foods are deep-fried in oil at lower temperatures for astonishingly long periods, resulting in a very dry and crispy end result. This is because a crispy texture is highly prized and is often held in higher esteem than the final taste. On the whole, recipes in this chapter call for the more conventional short fry at higher temperatures, but there are a few instances where I encourage frying at lower temperatures for longer periods to benefit the final texture of the dish.

I still find stir-fry dishes particularly exotic and exciting, not only to eat, but also to cook. The main reason for this is that these styles of dishes are cooked quickly at high temperatures, a somewhat foreign cooking method, and are generally always cooked in a wok. At the restaurant, we cook over turbo jets that burn at ferocious temperatures. Unfortunately, we don't have this luxury at home so the best thing to do is leave your wok over the highest heat for a long time until it gets as hot as possible. I cannot stress how important this is to achieve efficient stir-fry cooking at home, and, truth be told, it's near impossible to overheat your wok on a domestic home burner. To successfully stir-fry, you must flip and move (or stir) your ingredients around the wok to prevent them sticking and burning, while they pick up char and flavour from the wok's cooking surface. Due to this rapid cooking style, it's paramount to have all your ingredients prepped and ready to go. It is also useful to have liquid on hand, usually water or a light stock, for controlling the cooking temperature. They will help release foods that may have formed a crust with the wok's surface (essentially a deglazing process). All of the dishes in this chapter are measured as single portions, designed to serve one or two people. If you need to feed greater numbers, then prepare the food and cook in batches, so as to not overcrowd the wok, which would lower the temperature and affect the final result.

nahm pla waan pla tort

Whitebait in Fish Sauce Caramel

Nahm pla waan is a delicious sweet and salty sauce that literally translates as 'sweet fish sauce' and can be as simple as dissolving palm sugar in fish sauce. It is widely eaten in Thailand as a condiment for dipping fresh fruits, most commonly firm, tart unripe green mangoes. In many cases, cooks add more elaborate ingredients to flavour the sweet fish sauce, such as fried shallots, fried garlic and fried dried shrimp, which add depth and umami. I use *nahm pla waan* for all sorts of things at the restaurant, but this is one of my favourite combinations: crispy fried whitebait tossed with the sweet, salty caramel.

SERVES 2

5 tablespoons rice flour
1 teaspoon salt
1 teaspoon caster (superfine) sugar
300 g (10 oz) whitebait (fresh or frozen), or use another small fish such as sprats
vegetable oil, for deep-frying
1 teaspoon Toasted Chilli Powder (*prik bon*) (page 213)
1 lime, cut into wedges, to serve

For the sweet fish sauce (*nahm pla waan*)

250 g (9 oz/1½ cups) palm or brown sugar
2 tablespoons water
¼ teaspoon shrimp paste
3 tablespoons fish sauce
2.5 cm (1 in) piece of cassia bark, toasted
1 star anise, toasted
2 dried bird's eye chillies, toasted
1 tablespoon dried shrimp
1 tablespoon Fried Shallots (*hom jiaw*) (page 210)
1 tablespoon Fried Garlic (*gratiam jiaw*) (page 211)

For the sweet fish sauce, heat the palm sugar and water together in a large saucepan over a low heat until the sugar has completely dissolved. Add the shrimp paste, fish sauce, cassia bark, star anise and dried chillies, then bring to a simmer and cook for 5 minutes, or until slightly reduced. Test the consistency by spreading a small amount on a plate and chilling it in the refrigerator for a few minutes. The desirable consistency should be tacky and sticky but not too firm. Simmer for longer, or add water as necessary to achieve the right consistency.

Stir through the dried shrimp, Fried Shallots and Fried Garlic, then transfer to a container and leave to infuse for at least 2 hours before using (I prefer to leave the sauce to infuse for 24 hours for a better flavour). This recipe will make more than required but the sauce will keep indefinitely in an airtight container in the refrigerator. Remove from the refrigerator 1 hour before using to allow the caramel to come to room temperature, or warm gently in a pan to a pouring consistency.

When you're ready to cook, combine the rice flour, salt and caster sugar in a large bowl. Add the whitebait and toss well until coated in the flour mixture.

Pour the oil for deep-frying into a large wok to a depth of 10 cm (4 in) and heat until the oil reaches 170°C (340°F) on a cooking thermometer. Alternatively, drop a small cube of bread into the hot oil; if it turns golden brown in about 20 seconds, the oil is ready. Deep-fry the whitebait, working in batches, so you don't overcrowd the wok, for 5 minutes. The idea is to 'hard-fry' the whole fish so that they become very crispy and can be eaten whole.

Remove and drain well on a plate lined with paper towels.

Transfer the fried fish to a large bowl and drizzle over the sweet fish sauce, then sprinkle with the Toasted Chilli Powder. Toss the fried whitebait until well coated, then transfer to a serving plate with the lime wedges to squeeze over before eating.

gai tort
Thai Fried Chicken

Fried chicken is beloved in Thailand, as it is around the world, with cooks swearing that their recipe is better than the rest. What's certain is that Thai fried chicken is highly addictive and moreish, and is a particular weakness of mine. Thai chickens tend to be scrawny and tough compared to the fattened birds we have in Britain, so I look to buy smaller chickens when making this recipe. One of the first techniques that surprised me when I became a chef was the difference in flavour achieved by brining the meat – the simple method of submerging something in a salty solution means that the protein is seasoned throughout and retains its moisture after cooking. I now make the effort to always brine poultry at home, as I find the technique benefits lean birds that are in danger of drying out when cooked. Feel free to skip this initial step, but if you have never tried brining a chicken before, it's worth doing once to see what you are missing out on.

SERVES

50 g (2 oz/⅓ cup) salt, plus
    1 teaspoon extra
40 g (1½ oz/scant ¼ cup) caster
    (superfine) sugar
1 litre (34 fl oz/4 cups) water
outer husks and trimmings from
    6 lemongrass stalks, roughly
    chopped
3 tablespoons roughly chopped
    coriander (cilantro) stems
1 tablespoon Fried Garlic and
    Fragrant Garlic Oil (*gratiam jiaw*)
    (page 211)
1 whole chicken, about 2 kg (4 lb 8 oz)
2 tablespoons chopped coriander
    (cilantro) root or coriander stem
3 tablespoons chopped garlic
1 teaspoon white peppercorns
1 teaspoon black peppercorns
½ teaspoon ground turmeric
125 g (4 oz/¾ cup) rice flour
40 g (1½ oz/⅓ cup) tapioca flour
40 g (1½ oz/⅓ cup) tempura flour mix
    (Gogi brand) (if you can't find this,
    then double the quantity of tapioca
    flour)
1 tablespoon mild paprika
250 ml (9 fl oz/1 cup plus
    1 tablespoon) chilled sparkling
    water
vegetable oil, for deep-frying

First, make the brine by dissolving the 50 g (2 oz/⅓ cup) salt and the sugar in the water in a large container. Add the chopped lemongrass outer husks and trimmings, plus the coriander stems and any other aromatic trimmings you have, such as the thick inner stems from makrut lime leaves or the ends of shallots. Finally, add the Fried Garlic and Fragrant Garlic Oil and mix together well.

Break the chicken down by removing the legs and separating these into thighs and drumsticks, and removing the small drumsticks with wing tips. Remove the crown from the back section, then cut the crown down the middle to separate the two breasts. Leaving the breast meat on the bone, cut each breast into three pieces across the breastbone. Keep the backbone for stock (page 200). Submerge the chicken pieces in the brine, then leave in the refrigerator for 3 hours. Drain the chicken pieces and pat dry, discarding the used brine.

In a pestle and mortar, pound the coriander root, garlic, both types of peppercorns and the ground turmeric to a smooth paste. Massage this over the brined chicken pieces and refrigerate for another 3 hours. Remove the chicken from the refrigerator 1 hour before cooking, so the meat has time to come up to room temperature.

In a wide bowl, mix together all the flours, paprika and the 1 teaspoon of salt. Still whisking, gradually add the chilled sparkling water until you have a smooth batter with a consistency similar to that of pancake batter. Add the chicken pieces to the batter and submerge them so they are well coated. Leave the chicken pieces submerged in the batter for 15 minutes.

Pour the oil for deep-frying into a large wok to a depth of 10 cm (4 in) and heat until the oil reaches 170°C (340°F) on a cooking thermometer. Alternatively, drop a small cube of bread into the hot oil; if it turns golden brown in about 20 seconds, the oil is ready. Remove the chicken from the bowl of batter, shaking each piece to remove any excess, then carefully lower the chicken pieces into the hot oil, working in batches. Deep-fry for 6–8 minutes until golden brown and very crispy. Using tongs, transfer the chicken to a plate lined with paper towels or a wire rack while you fry the remainder of the chicken. Serve on a large platter.

SERVE WITH

- Sticky Rice (*khao neow*) (page 196)
- Shredded Vegetables with Spicy-sweet-sour-salty Dressing *(som tam)* (page 54)
- Sweet Chilli Sauce (*nahm jim gai waan*) (page 218)
- Grilled Long Chilli Relish (*nahm prik num*) (page 83)

Thai Fried Chicken

Fish Cakes with Cucumber Pickle

tort man pla

Fish Cakes with Cucumber Pickle

Thai fish cakes are famous around the world – and rightfully so, as their intriguingly bouncy texture and delicious flavour, with red curry paste running through the fish mixture, make them a delight to eat at any time of the day. I like to serve them as a snack or precursor to a meal with traditional sweet pickled cucumber, shallots and chillies known as *ajut* in Thailand. Fish cakes also make a wonderful light lunch served with a few coils of *kanom jim* rice vermicelli noodles and sprigs of Thai basil. If you don't have time to make the red curry paste, then use a good-quality shop-bought curry paste instead.

SERVES 6

2 tablespoons salt
2 tablespoons caster (superfine) sugar
300 g (10 oz) white fish, filleted with pin bones and skin removed (cod, hake and monkfish all work well)
1 teaspoon palm sugar
2 tablespoons fish sauce
1 large egg, beaten
3 tablespoons finely sliced fine green beans
1 tablespoon finely sliced fingerroot (optional)
8 makrut lime leaves (fresh or frozen), finely shredded
4 tablespoons large Thai basil leaves
vegetable oil, for deep-frying
dried vermicelli noodles, cooked according to packet instructions and cooled to room temperature
Thai basil or coriander (cilantro) sprigs

For the pickle, gently warm the vinegar, water, caster sugar and salt together in a small saucepan until the salt and sugar dissolve. Remove from the heat and leave until completely cold. In a small bowl, combine the cucumber, onion, chilli, ginger and coriander, then pour over the cold pickle liquid. Do this no more than 3 minutes before you plan to serve, as the vegetables will lose their crunch and texture as they sit in the pickle liquor.

For the curry paste, pound all the ingredients together in a stone pestle and mortar until very smooth (see pages 204–207 for an expanded explanation on efficiently pounding a curry paste).

In a small bowl, mix together the salt and sugar. This is your cure mix. Sprinkle it over the fish and leave for 1 hour in the refrigerator to draw the moisture from the fish. Wipe the cure mix from the fish and wash under cold running water, then pat dry with paper towels.

Traditionally, Thai fish cakes are made using a pestle and mortar, but for the modern cook, a food processor saves time. Cut the fish into bite-size pieces and add to the food processor, along with 4 tablespoons of the red curry paste, the palm sugar and fish sauce. Blend together well. Transfer to a large bowl and gradually incorporate the beaten egg so the fish mixture turns glossy and firm, yet sticky to the touch. Stir through the green beans, fingerroot and makrut lime leaves. Check the seasoning by frying a little of the mixture to taste: it should be aromatic and salty.

**For the cucumber pickle
(*ajut taeng kwaa*)**

4 tablespoons white wine vinegar
2 tablespoons water
3 tablespoons caster (superfine)
  sugar
½ tablespoon salt
¼ cucumber, quartered lengthways
  and cut into 5 mm (¼ in) slices
½ small red onion, sliced with the
  grain of the onion
1 long red chilli, sliced into rounds
1 tablespoon thinly shredded
  ginger root
1 tablespoon coriander (cilantro)
  leaves

**For the red curry paste (*khreuang
gaeng daeng*)**

6 dried long red chillies, seeded and
  soaked in cold water until soft
4 dried bird's eye chillies, soaked in
  cold water until soft
1 teaspoon salt
2 tablespoons thinly sliced
  lemongrass, root and outer
  husks removed
1 tablespoon chopped galangal
1 tablespoon chopped banana shallot
2 tablespoons chopped garlic
1 tablespoon chopped fingerroot (or
  use ginger root)
1 teaspoon makrut lime zest
1 teaspoon shrimp paste

Using wet hands, shape the mixture into 4 cm (1½ in) rustic discs, then place a Thai basil leaf around each fish cake so they are partially covered.

Pour the oil for deep-frying into a large wok to a depth of 10 cm (4 in) and heat until the oil reaches 180°C (350°F) on a cooking thermometer. Alternatively, drop a small cube of bread into the hot oil; if it turns golden brown in about 15 seconds, the oil is ready. Deep-fry the fish cakes, in batches, for 2 minutes until they float to the surface and are golden and slightly puffed. Remove and drain on a plate lined with paper towels, then repeat with the remaining fish cakes. Serve immediately with the rice vermicelli noodles, coiled and scattered with Thai basil or coriander (cilantro) sprigs.

SERVE WITH
- Sweet Chilli Sauce (*nahm jim gai waan*) (page 218)
- Roasted Chilli Jam (*nahm prik pao*) (page 82)

pad grapao neua

Stir-fried Minced Beef with Holy Basil

This is the ultimate Thai comfort food, and is one of my go-to Thai meals. It's highly addictive, so learning how to master it at home is a major blessing. The dish really encapsulates the subtle smoky flavour achieved from the *wok-hei* or 'breath of the wok' that cooks talk of when stir-frying. *Pad grapao* is deeply savoury, spicy and salty, with aromatic cassia notes from the lashings of holy basil leaves (*bai grapao*) used in the very best versions of the dish. In Thailand, this dish is commonly made with chopped beef, pork, chicken and seafood. It's one of those 'anything goes' sort of dishes, which is one of the reasons I love it so much. Holy basil isn't the easiest herb to source, but sweet Thai basil is popping up more and more on supermarket (grocery store) shelves, so if you see Thai basil, stock up with the aiming of making *pad grapao* – or what should actually be called *pad horapha*, meaning stir-fried Thai basil.

SERVES 2

2 tablespoons oyster sauce
1 tablespoon light soy sauce
1 tablespoon fish sauce
1 teaspoon caster (superfine) sugar
6 bird's eye chillies
2 tablespoons chopped garlic
1 teaspoon salt
6 tablespoons vegetable oil
2 large eggs
220 g (7½ oz/1 cup) minced (ground) beef
3 tablespoons fine green beans, cut into 3 cm (1¼ in) pieces
3 tablespoons Beef Stock (*nahm cheua neua*) (page 202) or water
40 g (1½ oz) holy or Thai basil, leaves picked

In a small bowl, combine the oyster sauce, soy sauce, fish sauce and sugar. This will be your seasoning sauce. It should taste savoury and salty, with a background sweetness. Set aside.

In a pestle and mortar, pound the chillies, garlic and salt together to a coarse paste. This will be your stir-fry paste. Set aside.

Heat the oil in a large wok over the highest possible heat until smoking hot. One at a time, crack the eggs into the hot oil and fry for 45 seconds until crispy on the bottom and edges. Spoon the hot oil over the eggs to cook the yolk, turning it opaque but keeping it runny. Set aside to drain on a plate lined with paper towels and keep warm while you cook the stir-fry.

Pour off and discard all but 2 tablespoons of the oil, then heat over a medium heat. Add the stir-fry paste and stir vigorously for about 30 seconds, or until the paste becomes fragrant. Increase the heat to high, then add the beef and stir-fry for 3 minutes, or until the beef is almost cooked through. Add the green beans and seasoning sauce. Continue to move the ingredients around in the wok for a further 1 minute so that the vegetables are tender but retain a bite and the beef is cooked through.

Add the stock and bring to the boil over a high heat. Check the seasoning; it should taste spicy and salty, with a slight background sweetness. If it tastes too intense, add a splash more stock. Add the basil leaves and toss everything together so the basil wilts. This is a holy basil stir-fry, after all, so be sure not to scrimp on the basil leaves. Serve immediately with the crispy fried eggs.

SERVE WITH

- Steamed Jasmine Rice (*khao hom mali*) (pages 194–195)
- Chilles soaked in Fish Sauce (*prik nahm pla*) (page 217)

pak kheo fai daeng

'Red Fire' Greens with Yellow Soybean Sauce

Traditionally, this dish is made using water spinach, sometimes referred to as morning glory. These tender leaves happily absorb the umami-rich flavours of the seasoning sauce. You can easily pick up water spinach in Asian supermarkets (grocery stores), but I prefer to use a selection of green vegetables based on what's in season. Use whatever works for you; just make sure to chop the vegetables into pieces that will cook evenly, as all the vegetables are stir-fried together. *Fai daeng* literally translates as 'red fire', which has nothing to do with the heat level or spice of the dish, but refers instead to the huge flame that leaps out of the wok as liquid hits the smoking-hot oil. I suggest not trying to replicate this step at home if you want to keep your eyebrows.

SERVES 2

2 tablespoons yellow soybean sauce

1½ tablespoons oyster sauce (omit for a vegetarian/vegan version)

½ tablespoon fish sauce (or use light soy sauce for a vegetarian/vegan version)

½ tablespoon caster (superfine) sugar

2 tablespoons chopped garlic

½ teaspoon salt

260 g (9 oz) mixed leafy greens, such as wild garlic leaves, spinach, mustard greens, watercress, turnip tops (*cime di rapa*), cabbage leaves and Brussels sprout tops

80 g (3 oz) green asparagus, sliced at an angle into 1 cm (½ in) pieces

2 red bird's eye chillies, bruised

2 tablespoons vegetable oil

100 ml (3½ fl oz/scant ½ cup) recently boiled Chicken Stock (*nahm cheua gai*) (page 200), or use Vegetable Stock (*nahm cheua jay*) (page 199) for a vegetarian/vegan version

In a small bowl, combine the yellow soybean sauce, oyster sauce, fish sauce and sugar. This is your seasoning sauce. Set aside.

In a pestle and mortar, pound the garlic and salt together to a coarse paste. Set aside.

In a large bowl, layer the vegetables from softest to hardest (i.e., start with spinach and wild garlic leaves, then turnip tops, cabbage leaves and asparagus). Top with the coarse garlic paste and the bruised bird's eye chillies.

Heat the oil in a large wok over a high heat until the oil is shimmering and approaching smoking point. Upturn the bowl of greens into the wok so that the paste, chillies and harder greens make direct contact with the hot surface of the wok. Leave them to char for 1 minute before stirring, flipping and mixing the vegetables so they wilt with the heat of the wok.

Add the stock and seasoning sauce and bring the stock to a fast boil, then toss together one final time. Taste the liquid: it should be well-seasoned and umami-rich with a background sweetness. Serve immediately, allowing the liquid to pool in the serving dish.

pad thai

Stir-fried Rice Noodles with Dried Prawns and Bean Sprouts

Pad thai could well be the most famous culinary export from Thailand, despite being a fairly recent addition to the Thai kitchen repertoire dating from the late 1930s. Over the years, the dish has been adapted to suit Western palates and the soul of the original dish has become lost along the way. It should come as no surprise that *pad thai* is a dish centred around noodles, and that the noodles should be the star of the show. In this instance, we use wide, flat rice noodles that go by the name 'rice sticks'. Look for Thai brands: you want a noodle that's 3 mm (⅛ in) wide. Aside from the noodles, there is a seasoning sauce that is equally sweet, tart and salty, while other staple ingredients include dried prawns (shrimp), firm tofu, salted radish and bean sprouts. These are all available at Asian supermarkets, and I recommend buying them the first time you cook this recipe so you can see how a true *pad thai* should taste, before making your own adjustments and substitutes. If you wish to add proteins to the recipe, then tiger prawns, chicken and pork are all fine choices, but their appearance in *pad thai* is something I associate with gentrified versions of the dish that take the focus away from the noodles.

SERVES 1

100 g (3½ oz) dried rice noodles (rice sticks)
2 tablespoons palm or brown sugar
2 tablespoons Tamarind Water (*nahm makham piak*) (page 214)
1 teaspoon white wine vinegar
2 tablespoons fish sauce
3 tablespoons chopped round shallot
1½ tablespoons chopped garlic
1 teaspoon salt
2–3 tablespoons rendered pork fat (page 216) or vegetable oil
1 large egg
2 tablespoons firm tofu, cut into 1 cm (½ in) dice
2 tablespoons dried shrimp, soaked for 5 minutes until tender, then drained well
1 tablespoon shredded salted radish (otherwise called preserved turnip; look for a Thai brand)
1 tablespoon roasted peanuts, coarsely crushed in a pestle and mortar
4 tablespoons (50 g/2 oz) bean sprouts, plus extra for sprinkling
2 tablespoons spring onions (scallions), cut into 3 cm (1¼ in) lengths
lime wedges, to serve

Soak the noodles in a large bowl of cold water for 20 minutes until they become soft and pliable, then rinse them of any starch under cold running and drain well.

In a bowl, stir together the sugar, Tamarind Water, vinegar and fish sauce until the sugar has completely dissolved. This is your *pad thai* seasoning sauce. Set aside.

In a pestle and mortar, pound the shallot, garlic and salt together to a coarse paste. Heat the pork fat or vegetable oil in a large wok over a medium heat, then add the paste and fry for 1 minute until fragrant and beginning to brown.

Crack the egg into the hot fat and stir so that the yolk breaks. Cook for 20–30 seconds until the egg resembles a soft omelette.

Add the drained noodles and stir to break up the egg, distributing it among the noodles. Add the seasoning sauce, along with the diced tofu, dried shrimp, shredded salted radish and crushed peanuts. Stir and toss all the ingredients well, then leave to simmer for 1 minute until almost all the sauce is absorbed and the noodles are completely tender.

Add the bean sprouts and spring onions, then toss and stir one final time so that all the ingredients are well combined and distributed. Transfer to serving plates and sprinkle with some more bean sprouts.

SERVE WITH
• Toasted Chilli Powder (*prik bon*) (page 213)

pad prik khing pla tort

Dry Red Curry of Crispy Salmon

Like many Thai dishes, *pad prik khing* indicates that this is a chilli (*prik*) stir-fry (*pad*) with ginger (*khing*). The first two assumptions are correct, but I've never come across a recipe for *pad prik khing* that includes ginger. Instead, this is a fragrant stir-fry or dry curry that is rich in flavour, due to the paste commonly being cooked out in rendered pork fat. Nowadays, most Thai cooks reach for a shop-bought red curry paste to cook this dish, and if you wish to do the same, then please do. My only recommendation would be that you adjust the paste slightly by pounding through some dried prawns (shrimp), as these will give the paste the extra dimension and richness needed for this dish.

SERVES 2

1 tablespoon fish sauce
½ teaspoon caster (superfine) sugar
160 g (5½ oz) salmon, fillet with skin
   on, sliced into 4 cm (1½ in) chunks
vegetable oil, for deep-frying
3 tablespoons rendered pork fat
   (page 216) or vegetable oil
1 tablespoon palm or brown sugar
3 makrut lime leaves (fresh or
   frozen), torn, plus 2 extra, finely
   shredded, to serve
2 tablespoons green peppercorn
   sprigs
2 tablespoons fine green beans, cut
   into 2 cm (¾ in) lengths
1 long red chilli, sliced on the
   diagonal into 1 cm (½ in) thick
   pieces
1 tablespoon sliced fingerroot (use
   the long slender part), optional

For the red curry paste
(khreuang gaeng daeng)

10 dried long red chillies, seeded
   and soaked in cold water until soft
1 teaspoon salt
2 tablespoons thinly sliced
   lemongrass, root and outer
   husks removed
2 tablespoons chopped galangal
1 tablespoon chopped coriander
   (cilantro) root or coriander stem
2 tablespoons chopped banana
   shallot
2 tablespoons chopped garlic
4 tablespoons dried shrimp, soaked
   until tender and drained well

For the curry paste, pound all the ingredients in a stone pestle and mortar until very smooth (see pages 204–207 for an expanded explanation on efficiently pounding a curry paste).

In a large bowl, mix together the fish sauce and caster sugar until the sugar has dissolved. Add the salmon to the bowl and leave to marinate for 5 minutes.

Pour the oil for deep-frying into a large wok to a depth of 8 cm (3 in) and heat until the oil reaches 165°C (330°F) on a cooking thermometer. Alternatively, drop a small cube of bread into the hot oil; if it turns golden brown in about 25 seconds, the oil is ready. Drain the salmon and carefully lower it into the hot oil, keeping the fish sauce marinade for later. Deep-fry the salmon for 5 minutes, or until crispy and dark golden. Remove the salmon and leave to drain on a plate lined with paper towels.

Pour off the oil and keep for another use. Add the pork fat or vegetable oil to the wok and warm over a medium heat. Add 2 tablespoons of the curry paste and stir-fry for 5 minutes, or until it smells fragrant, with a good sheen of oil. Add the palm sugar and reserved fish sauce marinade to season.

Add the crispy salmon to the wok, along with the torn makrut lime leaves, green peppercorns, green beans, sliced chilli and fingerroot, then gently toss and fold everything together to coat well with the seasoned curry paste. If the paste is too stiff and thick, then moisten with 1–2 tablespoons water, but be careful not to add too much liquid, as this should be a thick, dry sauce. It will taste rich and oily, with a well-seasoned salty and sweet background. Transfer to a serving dish and sprinkle with the shredded makrut lime leaves.

SERVE WITH

- Steamed Jasmine Rice (*khao hom mali*) (pages 194–195)
- Shiitake Mushroom and Thai Basil Soup with Tapioca Pearls (*gaeng jeut*) (page 102)
- Citrus-cured Tuna (*koi pla Isaan*) (page 57)

kua kling mu

Minced Pork Dry Turmeric Curry

This dry-style curry hails from Southern Thailand and holds all the classic characteristics of dishes from this region – hot and salty, with tones of fresh turmeric, lemongrass and makrut lime leaf. It's one of my favourite dishes to eat, but be warned: I've had versions before in Thailand that have nearly given me a nosebleed from the heavy use of chillies! I have pulled back the heat in this recipe, but only slightly, as the chilli spice is integral for a true *kua kling mu*. The dish is always eaten with freshly steamed jasmine rice and plenty of cooling vegetables to hand, like cucumber and cabbage.

SERVES 2

1 tablespoon vegetable oil
150 g (5 oz/⅔ cup) minced (ground) pork (not too fatty)
1 tablespoon fish sauce
½ teaspoon palm or brown sugar
2 tablespoons thinly sliced lemongrass, root and outer husks removed
3 tablespoons fine green beans, cut into 2 cm (¾ in) lengths
2 tablespoons green peppercorn sprigs
1 long red chilli, diagonally sliced into 1 cm (½ in) thick pieces
1 tablespoon bird's eye chillies (preferably small green *prik kii nuu suan*)
4 makrut lime leaves (fresh or frozen), finely shredded

For the southern Thai curry paste (*khreuang gaeng dtai*)

3 tablespoons dried bird's eye chillies, soaked in cold water for 15 minutes until soft
2 tablespoons thinly sliced lemongrass, root and outer husks removed
½ tablespoon chopped galangal
2 tablespoons chopped banana shallot
2 tablespoons chopped garlic
1 tablespoon chopped turmeric root or ½ tablespoon ground turmeric
½ tablespoon makrut lime zest
1 teaspoon shrimp paste
½ teaspoon black peppercorns
½ teaspoon salt

For the curry paste, pound all the ingredients together in a stone pestle and mortar until very smooth (see pages 204–207 for an expanded explanation on efficiently pounding a curry paste).

Heat the oil in a large wok over a low heat. Add the pork and 2 tablespoons of the curry paste, then mash and stir together allowing the curry paste and pork to combine and cook into each other. Once the pork is almost cooked through and the curry paste is no longer raw (about 5 minutes), season with the fish sauce and sugar.

Add the lemongrass, green beans, green peppercorn sprigs, chillies and half the shredded makrut lime leaves. Mix and mash the ingredients together so the green peppercorns and chilli bruise, releasing their heat. If the contents of the wok are catching too much and sticking, then moisten with 1 tablespoon of water at a time, ensuring the liquid evaporates so you are left with a dry curry. At this point, it will taste very spicy and salty, with a fragrance of lemongrass, makrut lime and turmeric. Transfer to a serving dish and sprinkle with the remaining shredded makrut lime leaves.

SERVE WITH

- Steamed Jasmine Rice (*khao hom mali*) (pages 194–195)
- Thai Omelette (*kai jiaw*) (page 90)

gaeng

Curries

I find the curries of Thailand the most fascinating of all the spectrum of dishes available. Thai curries range from the very simple to the incredibly complex. The most basic involve a few readily available and indigenous ingredients – a simple paste dissolved in stock (or sometimes only water), with the addition of local vegetables, foraged herbs and maybe a freshwater fish or rice paddy crabs. Thai curries are defined by the ingredients that make the curry paste, the way in which the curry paste is cooked out and seasoned, and the main ingredients in the final curry. Each of these three elements are of equal importance and should be well considered before embarking on cooking a curry, as the final dish will be influenced by all these aspects, which determine what type of curry it is.

Many people in Western culture are often surprised to hear that there are a wide variety of Thai curries that involve no coconut cream, assuming that this is a staple ingredient required for making these dishes. In fact, it's possible that stock-based curries are more widely eaten throughout Thailand than coconut cream curries, particularly the simple versions. Coconut cream is still a relatively premium ingredient to many Thai cooks living in Northern Thailand and Isaan. In these vast regions, the coconut palm is not an indigenous tree species, so coconut cream and coconut sugar rarely feature in traditional dishes from these areas.

For many cooks, rich coconut cream curries are the pinnacle of the Thai culinary repertoire, and rightly so, as they hold the most complexity – not only in the cooking technique, but also in their seasonings and the ingredients used. The majority of coconut cream curries hail from Central and Southern Thailand, where affluence is more apparent and the sheer number of indigenous coconut palm trees is vast. These more evolved curries implement complex cooking techniques and less abundant ingredients, ranging from the familiar green and red curries to the less known *gaeng gari* – an aromatic yellow curry that's rich and earthy with dried spices and turmeric. Coconut-based curries are fried in separated or 'cracked' coconut cream, giving them a richness of body and flavour (see page 209 for a note on separating coconut cream). The fried-out paste is then seasoned using palm sugar, fish sauce and sometimes tamarind water, to create an intense base of flavour before moistening with the cook's choice of coconut milk, stock or water, depending on the desired final curry.

gaeng om Isaan

Northeastern Curry of Trout and Leafy Greens

Gaeng om curries are from Thailand's northern provinces, with this particular recipe hailing from Isaan. The dish uses a rudimentary boiling method that is typical of the region, and always has a green or leafy vegetable as a featured ingredient – *om* is the Thai word for 'green leaf'. Curries of this style are very forgiving and accommodating when it comes to the ingredients used. Typically, any protein can be used, be it meat or fish, and these can be finely minced (ground), hand chopped or sliced, depending on the preference of the cook. Fermented fish sauce (*nahm pla raa*) is the preferred seasoning sauce of the region, but regular fish sauce makes for a more convenient and less pungent alternative. In keeping with traditional recipes, this curry has fresh dill running through it, which is sometimes referred to as Laos parsley in this part of the world. The dill brings a lovely bright and almost grassy flavour to the finished curry.

SERVES 4

500 ml (17 fl oz/2 cups) Fish Stock (*nahm cheua pla*) (page 203)
½ teaspoon caster (superfine) sugar
1½ tablespoons fish sauce
1 lemongrass stalk, cut into 6 cm (2½ in) batons and bruised
2 makrut lime leaves, fresh or frozen, torn
2 red bird's eye chillies, bruised
200 g (7 oz) leafy greens, preferably soft varieties such as spinach, watercress, turnip tops (*cime de rapa*) or wild garlic leaves
240 g (8½ oz) trout, filleted and cut into 5 cm (2 in) pieces on an angle
2 tablespoons Thai basil leaves
2 tablespoons tender dill tips

For the Isaan curry paste (*khreuang gaeng Isaan*)

1 tablespoon dried bird's eye chillies, soaked in cold water for 15 minutes until soft
3 tablespoons fresh red bird's eye chillies, chopped
½ teaspoon salt
1 tablespoon thinly sliced lemongrass, root and outer husks removed
½ tablespoon chopped galangal
1 tablespoon chopped turmeric root or ½ tablespoon ground turmeric
1 tablespoon chopped coriander (cilantro) root or coriander stem
2 tablespoons chopped banana shallot
2½ tablespoons chopped garlic
¾ tablespoon shrimp paste

For the curry paste, pound all the ingredients together in a stone pestle and mortar until very smooth (see pages 204–207 for an expanded explanation on efficiently pounding a curry paste).

Bring the stock to the boil in a large saucepan, then season with the sugar and fish sauce. Add the bruised lemongrass, makrut lime leaves and chillies, then add 2 tablespoons of the curry paste to the boiling stock and stir until it has dissolved.

Reduce the heat to a simmer and add the leafy greens and trout. Simmer for 1 minute until the greens are wilted and the trout is just cooked with a little pinkness in the middle. Remove from the heat and stir through the Thai basil leaves and half the dill. The curry should not be thin, and will taste salty, hot and slightly peppery from the greens and Thai basil. Transfer to a serving dish and finish by topping with the remaining dill.

SERVE WITH

- Steamed Jasmine Rice (*khao hom mali*) (pages 194–195) or Sticky Rice (*khao neow*) (page 196)
- Akhar Tribe Cashew and Dill Relish (*akhar sapi thong*) (page 85)
- 'Red Fire' Greens with Yellow Soybean Sauce (*pak kheo fai daeng*) (page 124)

gaeng lueng sapparot pla

Hot Turmeric Curry of Turbot and Pineapple

Gaeng lueng is Southern Thailand's version of the central region's Sour Orange Curry (*gaeng som*), with *lueng* meaning 'yellow' and *som* meaning 'orange'. The main difference is *gaeng lueng's* abundant use of fresh turmeric in its curry paste, as well as its aggressive seasoning, which leans towards Southern Thailand's love of very hot, sour and salty foods. The curry sauce is thin and almost brothy, but don't be fooled: it's packed full of vibrant flavour and chilli spice. In keeping with rural-style boiled curries, *gaeng lueng* is easy to prepare and cook. It is an incredibly versatile dish that works well with any fish or seafood, so don't feel restricted by my use of turbot in this version.

SERVES 2

160 g (5½ oz) semi-ripe pineapple
800 ml (27 fl oz/3½ cups) Fish Stock (*nahm cheua pla*) (page 203)
1 teaspoon caster (superfine) sugar
2 tablespoons fish sauce
2 tablespoons Tamarind Water (*nahm makham piak*) (page 214)
2 turbot steaks on the bone, about 200 g (7 oz) each
3 tablespoons lime juice

For the yellow curry paste (*khreuang gaeng lueng*)

3 tablespoons dried bird's eye chillies, soaked in cold water for 15 minutes until soft
1 teaspoon salt
1½ tablespoons chopped turmeric root
3 tablespoons chopped garlic
1 tablespoon chopped banana shallot
1 tablespoon shrimp paste

For the curry paste, pound all the ingredients together in a stone pestle and mortar until very smooth (see pages 204–207 for an expanded explanation on efficiently pounding a curry paste).

Peel and quarter the pineapple. Remove the core and set aside for another use (see Fermented Fish Sauce on page 215). Cut the pineapple flesh into 2.5 cm (1 in) pieces. Set aside.

Bring the stock to the boil in a large saucepan, then season with the sugar, fish sauce and Tamarind Water. Add 2 tablespoons of the curry paste and stir until it has dissolved into the stock, then simmer for 1 minute.

Add the turbot and pineapple and cook for 3 minutes until the turbot is just coming away from the bone and the pineapple is softened. Remove from the heat and finish the seasoning using the lime juice. The curry sauce should be thin and will taste very hot, sour and salty.

SERVE WITH

• Steamed Jasmine Rice (*khao hom mali*) (pages 194–195)

gaeng som pla

Sour Orange Sea Bass Curry

Gaeng som curries are some of the most popular among Thai people, with each household having their own recipe for the sour, warming and slightly sweet orange curry. The curry takes its name quite literally from the Thai word *som* – meaning both 'orange' and 'sour'. Similar to Southern Thailand's Hot Turmeric Curry (*gaeng lueng*) on page 138, these central-style sour orange curries are extremely versatile, using any combination of fish, seafood and vegetables to great effect.

SERVES 2

500 ml (17 fl oz/2 cups) Fish Stock (*nahm cheua pla*) (page 203)
250 g (9 oz) sea bass fillets, sliced into 5 cm (2 in) pieces
2 tablespoons fish sauce
1 teaspoon palm or caster (superfine) sugar
3 tablespoons Tamarind Water (*nahm makham piak*) (page 214)
50 g (2 oz) watercress

For the orange curry paste (*khreuang gaeng som*)

3 tablespoons dried bird's eye chillies, soaked in cold water for 15 minutes until soft
1 teaspoon salt
1 tablespoon chopped galangal
1 tablespoon chopped garlic
3 tablespoons chopped shallot
1½ tablespoons shrimp paste

For the curry paste, pound all the ingredients together in a stone pestle and mortar until very smooth (see pages 204–207 for an expanded explanation on efficiently pounding a curry paste). Set aside.

Bring the stock to the boil in a large saucepan, then reduce to a simmer and add the thinner tail and belly pieces of sea bass (about 70 g/2½ oz). Simmer for 1 minute until cooked through. Remove the fish with a slotted spoon and drain well, then flake into the curry paste. Gradually work the poached fish flesh into the curry paste with the pestle and mortar until smooth and completely incorporated. This will give the finished curry sauce a body and viscosity that would otherwise be missing.

Bring the stock back to the boil, then add the curry paste and stir until it has dissolved. Season with fish sauce, sugar and Tamarind Water. It will taste sour, spicy and salty, with a very slight background sweetness.

Add the remaining sliced sea bass pieces and the watercress and simmer for 1 minute until the fish is just cooked and the watercress is wilted. Transfer to a serving bowl and serve immediately.

SERVE WITH

- Steamed Jasmine Rice (*khao hom mali*) (pages 194–195)
- Pickled Vegetables (page 90)
- Thai Omelette (*kai jiaw*) (page 90)

gaeng ba hoi maeng phuu

Mussels in Pork Fat Jungle Curry

I have never encountered this dish or anything comparable in Thailand. This recipe came about when I first started cooking AngloThai pop-ups around the world. I'm a massive fan of jungle curries (*gaeng ba*) and wanted to find a way to give the spicy curry sauce additional body and depth. The introduction of pork fat not only serves this purpose, but it also gives the curry a lovely richness against the saline mussels. Other shellfish or fish such as clams, turbot and squid all work well with this sauce, so experiment to your heart's content.

SERVES 2

3 tablespoons rendered pork fat (page 216)
3 makrut lime leaves (fresh or frozen)
1 teaspoon palm or brown sugar
2 tablespoons fish sauce
500 g (1 lb 2 oz) live mussels, purged and cleaned
3 tablespoons Fish Stock (*nahm cheua pla*) (page 203) or water
30 g (1 oz) roughly chopped wild garlic leaves (if not in season, use Thai basil)

For the jungle curry paste (*khreuang gaeng ba*)

2 dried long red chillies, seeded and soaked in cold water for 15 minutes until soft
5 dried bird's eye chillies, soaked in cold water for 15 minutes until soft
1 teaspoon salt
3 tablespoons thinly sliced lemongrass, root and outer husks removed
1 tablespoon chopped galangal
1 tablespoon chopped coriander (cilantro) root or coriander stem
½ tablespoon chopped krachai (fingerroot) or wild ginger
1 tablespoon chopped turmeric root or ½ tablespoon ground turmeric
2 tablespoons chopped banana shallot
1½ tablespoons chopped garlic
1 tablespoon shrimp paste

For the curry paste, pound all the ingredients together in a stone pestle and mortar until very smooth (see pages 204–207 for an expanded explanation on efficiently pounding a curry paste).

Heat the pork fat in a large saucepan over a medium heat. Add the curry paste and cook, stirring frequently, for 2–3 minutes until fragrant and the rawness of the paste is cooked out. Add the makrut lime leaves and season with the sugar and fish sauce. Cook for another 5 minutes, then taste: it will be rich, spicy and salty.

Add the mussels and stock to the pan, then cover with a lid and gently swirl the pan around to combine the mussels with the jungle curry sauce, essentially emulsifying the curry paste and stock while coating the mussels in the process.

When the mussels are completely open, add the wild garlic leaves and gently fold together to wilt. Discard any mussels that are still closed and transfer to a serving bowl.

SERVE WITH

- Steamed Jasmine Rice (*khao hom mali*) (pages 194–195)
- Grilled Beef Ribeye with 'Waterfall' Salad (*neua yang nahm tok*) (page 68)
- Fragrant Shrimp and Coconut Cream Relish (*lon gapi*) (page 86)
- Deep-fried Vegetables (*pak tort*) (page 89)

gaeng hung lae

Burmese Pork Belly Curry with Pickled Garlic

This dish hails from Northern Thailand, around the major cities of Chiang Mai and Chiang Rai. As the name suggests, this recipe is influenced by neighbouring Myanmar (formerly Burma), with particular parallels seen from the heavy use of dried spices. *Gaeng hung lae* is rich, complex and one of my favourite curries during the colder months. Interestingly, the dish uses a combination of palm sugar, fresh ginger root, pickled garlic and tamarind to give it a warming, tart and sweet seasoning that is irresistible with the tender braised pork belly. Always make a large batch, as, like many curries, it gets better with time as the flavours develop and marry together.

SERVES 6

- 500 g (1 lb 2 oz) pork belly, cut into 4 cm (1½ in) cubes (this can include the pork ribs)
- 3 tablespoons black soy sauce or ketjap manis
- 3 tablespoons rendered pork fat (page 216) or fragrant garlic or shallot oil (pages 210 and 211)
- 1 tablespoon curry powder or shop-bought mild madras curry powder
- 3 tablespoons palm or brown sugar
- 3 tablespoons fish sauce
- 3 white cardamom pods, toasted
- 300 ml (10 fl oz/1¼ cups) Pork Stock (*nahm cheua mu*) (page 201)
- 15–20 small shallots, peeled (those used for pickling)
- 150 g (5 oz) piece of ginger root, peeled and coarsely shredded, plus 2 tablespoons finely shredded, to serve
- 150 g (5 oz) pickled garlic (peeled cloves)
- 4 tablespoons pickled garlic liquor
- 4 tablespoons Tamarind Water (*nahm makham piak*) (page 214)
- 3 tablespoons Fried Shallots (*hom jiaw*) (page 210)

For the curry paste, pound all the ingredients together in a stone pestle and mortar until very smooth (see pages 204–207 for an expanded explanation on efficiently pounding a curry paste). Set aside.

Wash the pork belly by following the instructions on page 105. If you prefer to skip this step, then this is fine; the cook time will be longer and the final sauce will be cloudy, but it will be equally delicious! Combine the drained pork belly with the black soy sauce, ensuring the meat is well coated.

Heat the pork fat or fragrant oil in a large wok over a medium heat. Add the curry paste and fry, stirring constantly, for 2–3 minutes until aromatic and fragrant. Add the curry powder and cook for 5 minutes until the mixture becomes darker and smells distinctly of the dried spices. Add the sugar, fish sauce, cardamom pods and blanched pork belly. Stir well to cover the pork belly with the seasoned curry paste, then add the stock. Bring to the boil, then reduce to a simmer and braise the pork belly for 30 minutes.

Add the shallots, coarsely shredded ginger, pickled garlic cloves, pickled garlic liquor and Tamarind Water and cook for another 45 minutes until the pork belly is tender and yielding, but retains its shape and is not completely collapsing in on itself. The curry will taste rich, salty, sweet and sour, with the warmth of ginger and dry spices. If serving immediately, transfer to a serving dish and top with the Fried Shallots and finely shredded ginger. Otherwise, leave to cool and keep for a day or two before reheating and serving with the accompaniments.

SERVE WITH

- Sticky Rice (*khao neow*) (page 196)
- Chiang Mai Herbal Sausage (*sai ua*) (page 70)
- Pork Scratchings (*khaep mu*) (page 91)

For the curry paste (*khreuang gaeng hung lae*)

10 dried long red chillies, seeded and soaked in cold water for 15 minutes until soft

1 teaspoon salt

3 tablespoons thinly sliced lemongrass, root and outer husks removed

1 tablespoon chopped galangal

2 tablespoons chopped ginger root

1 tablespoon chopped turmeric root or ½ tablespoon ground turmeric

4 tablespoons chopped banana shallot

4 tablespoons chopped garlic

1 tablespoon coriander seeds, toasted and ground to a fine powder

1 tablespoon cumin seeds, toasted and ground to a fine powder

3 star anise, toasted and ground to a fine powder

2.5 cm (1 in) piece of cassia bark, toasted and ground to a fine powder

4 cloves, toasted and ground to a fine powder

**For the red curry paste
(*khreuang gaeng daeng*)**
12 dried long red chillies, seeded
  and soaked in cold water for
  15 minutes until soft
1 teaspoon salt
2 tablespoons thinly sliced
  lemongrass, root and outer
  husks removed
1 tablespoon chopped galangal
1 teaspoon makrut lime zest
1 tablespoon chopped coriander
  (cilantro) root or coriander stem
6 tablespoons chopped shallot
4 tablespoons chopped garlic
1 teaspoon shrimp paste
2 tablespoons coriander seeds,
  toasted and ground to
  a fine powder
1 tablespoon cumin seeds,
  toasted and ground to
  a fine powder
½ teaspoon nutmeg, toasted and
  ground to a fine powder
1 teaspoon white peppercorns,
  ground to a fine powder

gaeng daeng bpet

Roast Duck and Lychee Red Curry

Gaeng daeng or red curries make up the largest range in the Thai culinary repertoire with their single most defining characteristic being that they are red in colour from the use of dried chillies. They are nearly always fried in separated coconut cream and can contain any number of protein and vegetable combinations. This recipe is a favourite of mine, and pairs roasted duck meat with sweet-tart lychees. The curry is married together in a sauce that is seasoned with fish sauce, palm sugar and a touch of tamarind water, and the resulting dish is complex and balanced.

SERVES 4

2 duck legs, about 135 g (4½ oz) each
1 tablespoon black soy sauce
1 duck breast, about 150 g (5 oz)
250 ml (9 fl oz/1 cup plus
   1 tablespoon) coconut cream
   (the richer, heavier solids that rise to
   the top of the thinner milk)
2 tablespoons palm or brown sugar
1 tablespoon fish sauce
1 tablespoon Tamarind Water
   (*nahm makham piak*) (page 214)
150 ml (5 fl oz/⅔ cup) coconut milk
250 ml (9 fl oz/1 cup plus
   1 tablespoon) Chicken Stock (*nahm
   cheua gai*) (page 200)
100 g (3½ oz) lychees (fresh or
   canned; rinse off the sweet syrup
   if using canned)
4 makrut lime leaves (fresh or
   frozen), torn
3 tablespoons Thai basil leaves

SERVE WITH

- Steamed Jasmine Rice (*khao hom
  mali*) (pages 194–195)
- Pickled Vegetables (*pak dong*)
  (page 90)

Preheat the oven to 170°C (340°F/gas 3). To make the curry paste, pound all the ingredients together in a stone pestle and mortar until very smooth (see pages 204–207 for an expanded explanation on efficiently pounding a curry paste). Set aside. Alternatively, use a good-quality shop-bought red curry paste.

Rub the duck legs with the black soy sauce and roast in the oven for 45 minutes until the meat is tender and the fat has rendered. Meanwhile, score the skin on the duck breast and place in a cold pan, skin-side down. Place over a low–medium heat and allow the fat to slowly render out from the duck skin for about 5 minutes. After this time, there should be a noticeable amount of fat rendered and the skin will be golden brown and crisp. Transfer to the oven with the legs and roast for 5 minutes, then remove the breast from the oven and leave it to rest. This should produce a blushing pink breast, but if it's not completely cooked through at this stage, it doesn't matter, as you can finish cooking it in the curry sauce later.

Combine the thick coconut cream with 2 tablespoons of the rendered duck fat in a saucepan. Warm over a medium heat for 3 minutes, or until the cream separates, the thinner liquid evaporates, and the surface develops an oily sheen (see page 209). Add 3 tablespoons of the curry paste and cook, stirring, until it is completely incorporated with the cream. Continue to fry for another 5 minutes until the mixture darkens and becomes fragrant. This indicates the rawness from the curry paste has been cooked out. Season with the sugar, fish sauce and Tamarind Water, then add the coconut milk and the stock. Bring to the boil, then reduce to a simmer and cook for another 8 minutes until the sauce develops an oily sheen on the surface.

Add the lychees and makrut lime leaves and continue to simmer for 1 minute. Flake the duck legs into bite-size pieces and cut the breast into 2.5 cm (1 in) slices. Add these to the curry, along with the Thai basil, and warm through in the curry sauce. If the duck breast is already cooked to your liking, then add it last to avoid overcooking the breast. The curry will taste rich, salty, sweet and slightly tart. Transfer to a serving bowl and top with a splash of thick coconut cream.

gaeng panang neua

Peanut-enriched Curry of Beef Cheek and Thai Basil

Generally speaking, *gaeng panang* is a variation of red curry where the paste is enriched with peanuts. The flavours dance between salty, sweet and aromatic, with a pleasing, rich, peanutty background flavour. For a lighter-style curry, boil the peanuts in coconut cream before cooling and pounding into the paste. Alternatively, roast the peanuts to give the final curry a toasted and deeply savoury peanut flavour. *Gaeng panang* tends to be made with beef that has been braised until tender in coconut milk. I have chosen beef cheek in tribute to a version we used to cook at Som Saa, but short rib, shank or brisket would all work wonderfully. Don't scrimp on the Thai basil, as this imparts a sweet anise floral element that is paramount in this curry.

SERVES 4

6 tablespoons raw skinless peanuts
800 ml (27 fl oz/3½ cups) coconut milk
400 g (14 oz) beef cheek, sinew and silver skin removed, cut into 6 cm (2½ in) chunks
offcuts of lemongrass from curry paste, roughly chopped
3 tablespoons coriander (cilantro) root or coriander stem
6 makrut lime leaves (fresh or frozen), 4 left whole and 2 torn
2.5 cm (1 in) piece of cassia bark, toasted
½ tablespoon salt
300 ml (10 fl oz/1¼ cups) coconut cream (the richer, heavier solids that rise to the top of the thinner milk), plus extra to finish
2 tablespoons coconut oil
1½ tablespoons palm sugar
2 tablespoons fish sauce
2 long red or green chillies, sliced on the diagonal into 4 cm (1½ in) lengths
6 tablespoons Thai basil leaves
2 tablespoons roasted peanuts, lightly crushed

To make the curry paste, pound all the ingredients together in a stone pestle and mortar until very smooth (see pages 204–207 for an expanded explanation on efficiently pounding a curry paste).

Put the peanuts and coconut milk into a large saucepan and bring to the boil. Boil for about 30 minutes, or until the nuts are very soft. Drain and leave to cool completely, keeping the coconut milk aside for the main curry. Alternatively, preheat the oven to 170°C (340°F/gas 3) and roast the peanuts in the oven for 10 minutes, or until golden brown. Add the cooked peanuts to the curry paste and pound until very smooth and completely incorporated. Set aside. Alternatively, use a good-quality shop-bought panang paste or add roasted peanuts to a good-quality shop-bought red curry paste.

Put the beef cheek into a large saucepan with the lemongrass offcuts, coriander root, whole makrut lime leaves, cassia bark, reserved coconut milk and salt. Bring to a quick boil, then reduce to a simmer. Cover the pan and cook for 2 hours, or until the beef cheeks are tender but retain their shape. Strain the beef cheeks, retaining the meat and braising liquor, but discarding the aromatic ingredients.

Combine the thick coconut cream with the coconut oil in a heavy-based saucepan and warm over a medium heat for about 3 minutes, or until the cream separates, the thinner liquid evaporates, and the surface develops an oily sheen (see page 209). Add 4 tablespoons of the curry paste and cook for 3–5 minutes, or until completely incorporated with the coconut cream. Fry for another 8 minutes, or until the mixture darkens and becomes fragrant. Season with the sugar and fish sauce, allowing these to cook into the paste before adding the reserved braising liquor and the torn makrut lime leaves. The braising liquor makes the curry very beefy in flavour, so, if you prefer, you can use fresh coconut milk for a lighter final dish, or a combination of the two: use your judgement after tasting the braising liquor.

**For the panang curry paste
(khreuang gaeng panang)**

8 dried long red chillies, seeded and
  soaked in cold water for 15 minutes
  until soft
1 teaspoon salt
2 tablespoons thinly sliced
  lemongrass, root and outer
  husks removed
1½ tablespoons chopped galangal
1 teaspoon makrut lime zest
1 tablespoon chopped coriander
  (cilantro) root or coriander stem
4 tablespoons chopped banana
  shallot
2 tablespoons chopped garlic
1 teaspoon shrimp paste, dry-toasted
  in banana leaf or foil (see page 168)
1½ tablespoons coriander
  seeds, toasted and ground to
  a fine powder
1½ tablespoons cumin seeds, toasted
  and ground to a fine powder
1 teaspoon nutmeg, toasted and
  ground to a fine powder

Add the sliced chillies and reserved beef cheek to the curry, warming the meat through for 1–2 minutes and cooking the chillies so they lose their bite. Finish the curry by folding through the Thai basil, then transfer to a serving dish and top with a splash of thick coconut cream before sprinkling over the crushed roasted peanuts. The final curry should be quite thick and oily and should taste rich and salty, sweet and complex.

SERVE WITH
• Steamed Jasmine Rice (khao hom mali) (pages 194–195)
• Pickled Vegetables (pak dong) (page 90)

Peanut-enriched Curry of Beef Cheek and Thai Basil

Roast Celeriac Curry with Whole Makrut Lime

gaeng tay po

Roast Celeriac Curry with Whole Makrut Lime

This unique *gaeng krua* uses the whole makrut lime fruit, giving a brightly flavoured coconut cream curry that feels lighter and fresher in comparison to more commonly known red curries. The final seasoning is tart, sweet and salty, which makes for an interesting eating experience. I really like celeriac (celery root) for its sweet and earthy tones, and they marry well with this curry. I served a version of this recipe during a residency where the only cooking equipment was a charcoal grill, which meant baking the celeriac in the dying embers at the end of each service. In this recipe, I've opted for an easier technique of roasting the celeriac in the oven, but if you want to experiment by baking the root vegetable in charcoal embers, this will definitely add to the depth of flavour in the final dish. Omit the shrimp paste and substitute fish sauce for light soy sauce to make this recipe vegetarian/vegan.

SERVES 6

600 ml (20 fl oz/2½ cups) coconut cream (the richer, heavier solids that rise to the top of the thinner milk), plus extra splash to finish

1 tablespoon salt

1 small (500 g/1 lb 2 oz) celeriac (celery root), peeled and cut into 5cm (2 in) pieces

1 tablespoon coconut oil

2 tablespoons palm sugar

1 tablespoon fish sauce

200 ml (7 fl oz/scant 1 cup) coconut milk

200 ml (7 fl oz/scant 1 cup) Vegetable Stock (*nahm cheua jay*) (page 199) or water

2 long red or green chillies, sliced on the diagonal into 4 cm (1½ in) lengths

2 makrut lime leaves (fresh or frozen), torn

1 makrut lime, halved or use regular lime

2 tablespoons Tamarind Water (*nahm makham piak*) (page 214)

100 g (3½ oz) wild garlic leaves or another soft leaf, such as spinach

Preheat the oven to 190°C (375°F/gas 5). To make the curry paste, pound all the ingredients together in a stone pestle and mortar until very smooth (see pages 204–207 for an expanded explanation on efficiently pounding a curry paste). Set aside. Alternatively, use a good-quality shop-bought red curry paste.

Combine half of the thick coconut cream with the salt in a large saucepan, then bring to the boil and boil for 2–3 minutes, or until reduced by a quarter. Coat the celeriac in this salted coconut cream and place on a roasting tray. Roast for 30 minutes, or until golden and completely cooked through, basting the celeriac with the salted cream every 10 minutes as it cooks. This will build a lovely crust on the celeriac and aids the natural caramelisation.

Combine the remaining thick coconut cream with the coconut oil in another large saucepan and warm over a medium heat for 3 minutes, or until the cream separates, the thinner liquid evaporates, and the surface develops an oily sheen (see page 209). Add 3 tablespoons of the curry paste and cook for another 5 minutes until it is completely incorporated with the cream. Season with the sugar and fish sauce, then add the coconut milk and stock. Bring to a simmer and cook for another 5 minutes until the sauce develops a slight oily sheen on the surface.

Add the roasted celeriac, along with the sliced chillies, makrut lime leaves and halved makrut lime. Cook for a few minutes so the makrut lime imparts its citrus flavour to the curry, giving a pleasant tart brightness to the sauce. Be sure not to over-boil or stew the makrut lime, or it will become bitter and unpleasant.

For the curry paste (*khreuang gaeng tay po*)

10 dried long red chillies, seeded and soaked in cold water for 15 minutes until soft
1 teaspoon salt
2 tablespoons thinly sliced lemongrass, root and outer husks removed
1 tablespoon chopped galangal
1 teaspoon makrut lime zest
1 tablespoon chopped coriander (cilantro) root or coriander stem
3 tablespoons chopped banana shallot
2 tablespoons chopped garlic
1 teaspoon shrimp paste
½ teaspoon coriander seeds, toasted and ground to a fine powder
½ teaspoon white peppercorns, ground to a fine powder

Remove from the heat and leave the curry to stand for a few minutes so the flavours can develop. Add the Tamarind Water to give a final seasoning of tart and sweet with saltiness in the background. Finish with the wild garlic leaves, stirring to wilt in the residual heat of the curry. Transfer to a serving dish, top with a splash of thick coconut cream and serve.

SERVE WITH
- Steamed Jasmine Rice (*khao hom mali*) (pages 194–195)
- Pickled Vegetables (*pak dong*) (page 90)

For the green curry paste (*khreuang gaeng kheo*)

2 long green chillies, seeded
6 green bird's eye chillies, chopped
1 teaspoon salt
2 tablespoons thinly sliced lemongrass, root and outer husks removed
1 tablespoon chopped galangal
1 teaspoon chopped turmeric root or ¼ teaspoon ground turmeric
1 teaspoon makrut lime zest
1 tablespoon chopped coriander (cilantro) root or coriander stem
3 tablespoons chopped banana shallot
2 tablespoons chopped garlic
1 teaspoon shrimp paste
1 teaspoon coriander seeds, toasted and ground to a fine powder
½ teaspoon cumin seeds, toasted and ground to a fine powder
1 teaspoon white peppercorns, ground to a fine powder

gaeng kheo wan luk chin pla

Fish Ball Green Curry

Thai green curry is possibly the most famous of all the curries and is found on Thai restaurants' menus across the world. The curry takes its colour from the use of fresh green chillies, which also give the dish its sharp spiciness – a characteristic that has been sacrificed in Western versions in favour of crowd-pleasing sweetness and cloying amounts of coconut cream. Purists add no sugar to the curry, instead relying on the natural sweetness of the fresh coconut cream to mitigate the heat of the chillies. Lemongrass, galangal and makrut lime give the curry paste an aromatic property, and the addition of fresh turmeric root not only provides earthiness, but also helps accentuate the vibrant colour of the final curry.

SERVES 6

250 ml (9 fl oz/1 cup plus
  1 tablespoon) coconut cream
  (the richer, heavier solids that rise to
  the top of the thinner milk)
1 tablespoon coconut oil
½ teaspoon palm sugar
2 tablespoons fish sauce
150 ml (5 fl oz/⅔ cup) coconut milk
200 ml (7 fl oz/scant 1 cup) Fish Stock
  (*nahm cheua gai*) (page 203)
4 makrut lime leaves (fresh or
  frozen), torn
6 green asparagus spears
  (100 g/3½ oz), cut into 2.5 cm
  (1 in) lengths
2 long red or green chillies, sliced
  on the diagonal into 5 cm (2 in)
  lengths
3 tablespoons Thai basil leaves

For the fish balls (*luk chin pla*)

2 tablespoons chopped coriander
  (cilantro) root or coriander stem
2 tablespoons chopped garlic
1 tablespoon chopped ginger root
1 teaspoon salt
½ teaspoon white peppercorns
2 tablespoons fish sauce
1 teaspoon caster (superfine) sugar
3 tablespoons tapioca flour
300 g (10½ oz) cod fillet, skin
  removed and chopped

To make the fish balls, pound the coriander root, garlic, ginger, salt and white peppercorns in a pestle and mortar until very smooth. Combine the paste with the fish sauce, caster sugar, tapioca flour and cod, then blend the mixture thoroughly in a food processor for 2 minutes until well combined. The mixture should feel smooth and bouncy. Using wet hands, shape the mixture roughly into 2.5 cm (1 in) balls. Bring a large saucepan of salted water to a low simmer, then add the fish balls and gently poach for 3 minutes, or until cooked through. The fish balls will float to the surface when they are cooked. Drain and set aside.

To make the curry paste, pound all the ingredients together in a stone pestle and mortar until very smooth (see pages 204–207 for an expanded explanation on efficiently pounding a curry paste). Set side. Alternatively, use a good-quality shop-bought green curry paste with 1 teaspoon of ground turmeric added to make the final colour more vibrant.

Combine the thick coconut cream with the coconut oil in a large saucepan over a medium heat and cook for about 2 minutes, or until the cream separates, the thinner liquid evaporates, and the surface develops an oily sheen (see page 209). Add 4 tablespoons of the curry paste and cook for 5 minutes until completely incorporated and the mixture darkens, becoming fragrant. Season with the palm sugar and fish sauce, allowing these to cook into the paste, before adding the coconut milk, stock and torn makrut lime leaves. At this stage, it should taste spicy, salty and aromatic.

Bring the curry sauce to a simmer, then add the asparagus, chillies and fish balls. Simmer for 1 minute so the vegetables retain their crispness, while warming the fish balls through. Stir in the Thai basil and transfer to a serving dish.

SERVE WITH

- Steamed Jasmine Rice (*khao hom mali*) (pages 194–195)
- Pickled Vegetables (*pak dong*) (page 90)

gaeng massaman neua

Muslim-spiced Curry of Beef Short Rib

Massaman is a widely recognised curry, but most traditional Thai recipes I've encountered are highly time-consuming and complex compared to simpler versions we encounter in Britain. Don't let that put you off, as the rewards are great for those wanting to make this Muslim-Thai curry at home. The curry paste requires dry-toasting of the aromatic ingredients and uses various dried spices to bring deep layers of flavour to the final dish. This is probably the most complex and labour-intensive recipe in the book, but it certainly makes for a good rainy-day activity – or, if you prefer to break down the main jobs over a couple of days, that will make it more achievable.

SERVES 8

1 kg (2 lb 4 oz) beef short rib, cut into 10 cm (4 in) pieces by your butcher
3 tablespoons fish sauce
1 litre (34 fl oz/4 cups) coconut milk
8 cm (3 in) piece of cassia bark, toasted
2 star anise, toasted
4 white cardamom pods, toasted
1 dried mandarin peel (see page 34)
2 bay leaves (fresh or frozen)
6–8 medium Jersey Royal potatoes (350 g/12 oz), peeled
200 ml (7 fl oz/scant 1 cup) coconut cream (the richer, heavier solids that rise to the top of the thinner milk), plus an extra splash to finish
2 tablespoons palm sugar
2 tablespoons fish sauce
3 tablespoons jumbo golden sultanas (golden raisins)
2 tablespoons Tamarind Water (*nahm makham piak*) (page 214)
2 tablespoons Fried Shallots (*hom jiaw*) (page 210)

salt

Preheat the oven to 160°C (320°F/gas 2). To make the curry paste, add the lemongrass, galangal, ginger, coriander root, shallot and garlic to a wok over a medium heat and dry-toast for 10 minutes to give colour and evaporate some of the water content from the ingredients. This will concentrate the flavour and give a roasted, smoky taste. Transfer to a stone pestle and mortar and pound until smooth, then add the remaining curry paste ingredients. (See pages 204–207 for an expanded explanation on efficiently pounding a curry paste.) Set aside.

Roll the beef short rib in the fish sauce, then place in a hot, dry pan over a high heat for 5 minutes to sear. This will give a golden colour and crust to the outside of the meat. There should be enough fat in the short rib to prevent it from sticking to the pan. Set aside and reserve the rendered fat.

In a large saucepan, combine the coconut milk, cassia bark, star anise, white cardamom pods, dried mandarin peel and bay leaves. Bring to the boil, then set aside.

Add the beef pieces to an ovenproof casserole dish with a tight-fitting lid, then cover with the coconut milk and whole spices. Cover with a lid, then braise in the oven for 2 hours, or until tender. The beef should be soft and falling from the bone, but without completely collapsing on itself.

Strain the braising liquor and set aside; you should have about 500 ml (17 fl oz/2 cups). Leave the beef to cool slightly before slicing into 2.5 cm (1 in) pieces.

Add the potatoes to a large saucepan and cover with lightly salted water. Bring to the boil, then reduce the heat and simmer for 8–10 minutes until cooked through. Strain and set aside.

**For the massaman curry paste
(*khreuang gaeng massaman*)**

3 tablespoons thinly sliced
   lemongrass, root and outer
   husks removed
2 tablespoons chopped galangal
1 tablespoon chopped ginger root
4 tablespoons chopped banana
   shallot
4 tablespoons chopped garlic
1 tablespoon chopped coriander
   (cilantro) root or coriander stem
10 dried long red chillies, seeded and
   soaked in cold water for 15 minutes
   until soft
1 teaspoon salt
½ tablespoon shrimp paste, toasted
   in banana leaf or foil (see page 168)
1 teaspoon coriander seeds, toasted
   and ground to a fine powder
½ teaspoon cumin seeds, toasted
   and ground to a fine powder
2 cloves, toasted and ground to a fine
   powder
1 mace sheath, toasted and ground
   to a fine powder
½ teaspoon nutmeg, toasted and
   ground to a fine powder
½ teaspoon white peppercorns,
   ground to a fine powder

Combine the thick coconut cream with the reserved rendered fat in another large saucepan and warm over a medium heat for 3 minutes, or until the cream separates, the thinner liquid evaporates, and the surface develops an oily sheen (see page 209). Add 4 tablespoons of the curry paste and cook for another 5 minutes until it is completely incorporated with the coconut cream. Fry for about 8 minutes, or until the mixture darkens and becomes fragrant, then season with the sugar and fish sauce, allowing these to cook into the paste before adding the reserved braising liquor. Bring to a simmer and cook for another 8–10 minutes until the sauce develops an oily sheen on the surface.

At this point, you should have a sauce of pouring consistency, which is rich in aroma and colour, and tastes sweet, rich and complex thanks to the dried spices. Add the sliced beef short rib to the sauce, along with the sultanas and cooked potatoes, and warm all the ingredients together for 1 minute. Remove from the heat and leave to stand for 5 minutes so the flavours can develop. Add the Tamarind Water to lighten the seasoning and add a slightly fresh taste to the final curry – it should be sweet, sour and salty. Transfer to a serving dish and top with a splash of coconut cream and the Fried Shallots.

SERVE WITH

- Steamed Jasmine Rice (*khao hom mali*) (pages 194–195)
- Pickled Vegetables (*pak dong*) (page 90)

Muslim-spiced Curry of Beef Short Rib

Curried Fish Mousse Steamed in Banana Leaf

hor mok pla

Curried Fish Mousse Steamed in Banana Leaf

This recipe pairs meaty white fish, such as pollock or cod, with an aromatic curry paste, coconut cream and herbs to give a delicate steamed curry parcel with a light mousse texture. I personally love the fish version of *hor mok*, but it's also possible to use chicken breast or other seafood to make the mousse. In Thailand, *hor mok* parcels are steamed in banana leaves, but I realise that it may be difficult to source banana leaves here so filling ramekins before steaming will give the same results. This recipe is very dear to me as it's the first Thai dish I cooked for my wife Desiree.

SERVES 2

260 g (9 oz) skinless cod fillet (or any other meaty white fish), pin bones removed, cut into small pieces

100 g (3½ oz/scant ½ cup) coconut cream (the richer, heavier solids that rise to the top of the thinner milk), plus extra to serve

1 teaspoon palm or brown sugar

2 tablespoons fish sauce

1 large egg, beaten

4 banana leaves, cut into 20 × 20 cm (8 × 8 in) squares (alternatively, use ramekins)

2–3 tablespoons Thai basil leaves

30 g (1 oz) roughly chopped wild garlic leaves or three-cornered leeks (if in season)

1 long red chilli, finely shredded

2 makrut lime leaves (fresh or frozen), finely shredded

For the red curry paste (*khreuang gaeng daeng*)

10 dried long red chillies, seeded and soaked in cold water for 15 minutes until soft

1 teaspoon salt

2 tablespoons thinly sliced lemongrass, root and outer husks removed

1 tablespoon chopped galangal

1 teaspoon makrut lime zest

1 tablespoon chopped coriander (cilantro) root or coriander stem

2½ tablespoons chopped shallot

2½ tablespoons chopped garlic

1 teaspoon shrimp paste

To make the curry paste, pound all the ingredients together in a stone pestle and mortar until very smooth (see pages 204–207 for an expanded explanation on efficiently pounding a curry paste). Set aside. Alternatively, use a good-quality shop-bought red curry paste.

Add the fish and a splash of the thick coconut cream to a food processor, along with the sugar, fish sauce and 3 tablespoons of the red curry paste. Blend together, gradually adding the remaining coconut cream until you have a smooth and glossy mixture. Blending will develop the proteins in the fish and will create a light and bouncy texture. Next, still blending, gradually incorporate the beaten egg. The final mixture should be silky and glossy, with a little wobble. Fry or poach a small amount of the mixture in oil and taste for seasoning; it should be salty, slightly sweet and rich.

If using banana leaves, you will need to make the leaves malleable so they don't tear when being folded. To do this, simply pass the banana leaf squares over an open flame on your hob. The leaf will change colour when it's fully malleable and will be flexible to fold.

Lay a square of banana leaf on your work surface, shiny-side down, then lay another on top but with the seam lines running in the opposite direction, again shiny-side down. Place a generous amount of Thai basil and wild garlic leaves, if using, in the centre of the banana leaf, then spoon a quarter of the curry fish mixture on top of the herbs, then add another generous amount of herbs on top so that the curry mixture is partially covered. Seal the mixture in the banana leaf by folding up the sides to create a tightly folded rectangle. The parcel should hold together if you turn the seam-side down on to the work surface. Repeat to make 4 parcels in total. If you are struggling to seal the parcels, you may have too much mixture inside. If you prefer, you can secure the banana leaf together using a few cocktail sticks (toothpicks).

Steam the banana leaf parcels over gently rolling water. I use a bamboo steamer, but a metal steamer works fine. Depending on the size of the parcels, they will take 12–15 minutes. To check if they're cooked, insert the tip of a sharp knife into the centre of the steamed fish mixture. Leave the knife in for a few seconds before removing; it should be hot to the touch and clean of fish mixture. Steam for a little longer if necessary.

The parcels will release liquid as they steam, so gently open the parcel and drain off any excess liquid from inside. Serve immediately, garnished with a splash of the remaining thick coconut cream, and with the shredded chilli and makrut lime leaves sprinkled over.

Cook's note: If you are not using banana leaves, then skip those steps and instead fill the base of two small ramekins with the herbs, then top with the fish mixture, followed by more herbs. Seal the ramekins with clingfilm (plastic wrap) so they are watertight when you steam the mixture.

SERVE WITH

- Steamed Jasmine Rice (*khao hom mali*) (pages 194–195)
- Fried Egg Salad (*yum khai dao*) (page 46)
- Pickled Vegetables (*pak dong*) (page 90)

gap glaeem

Snacks

The culture of snacking in Thailand has always existed and is considered as important as standard mealtimes, with long discussions surrounding the merits of particular dishes compared to others – taking place, of course, while snacking on the foods in question. For many, snacking is not only for nourishment, but is also an enjoyable activity to whittle away spare time – and Thailand is well suited for it, with the plethora of food vendors littering the streets, each with their own tasty morsels on sale for affordable prices. Despite this love of snacking, there is no traditional culture of eating appetisers before meals like we do in the Western world. However, I feel that many bite-size snacks from the Thai repertoire do an excellent job of whetting the appetite before a wider meal. A nugget of sweet, salty and nutty caramelised meat sitting atop a refreshing piece of fruit (*ma hor*), or a plump oyster topped with a tangy sea buckthorn dressing (*hoi naang rohm*) are fine beginnings to any number of meals. Of course, don't just eat these dishes as precursors to meals; it would be equally agreeable to prepare a selection of these recipes as finger food with a chilled glass of pét-nat wine or an ice-cold beer. There are no set rules, so have fun with the recipes that follow.

ponlamai prik gleua

Fruits with Salty-sweet Chilli Dip

These dips are versions of the salt, sugar and chilli condiment that Thai fruit vendors sell alongside seasonal fresh fruits for dipping. Most versions I've encountered use a blend of sugar, salt and toasted chilli powder (*prik bon*) for a rustic dip that enhances the flavours of the fruits. I've also included a version I serve at the restaurant, which uses small green chillies called *prik kii nuu suan*. The chillies have a wonderful fruity, spicy flavour and, when coupled with lemon verbena leaves, the end result is a vibrant salty-sweet chilli mix that works brilliantly with fresh, tart unripe Granny Smith apples.

SERVES 6

sliced, under-ripe raw fruit, such as apple, pear, plum and rhubarb

For the Bangkok-style dip

90 g (3¼ oz/⅓ cup plus 2 teaspoons) caster (superfine) sugar
1 tablespoon fine salt
1 teaspoon Toasted Chilli Powder (*prik bon*) (page 213)

For the AngloThai-style dip

2 tablespoons lemon verbena leaves
1 tablespoon chopped coriander (cilantro) root or coriander stem
2 tablespoons chopped green bird's eye chillies (*prik kii nuu suan*) or small green Indian chillies
1 teaspoon makrut lime zest or lime zest
1 tablespoon fine salt
90 g (3¼ oz/⅓ cup plus 2 teaspoons) caster (superfine) sugar

For the Bangkok-style dip, mix together all the ingredients in a stone mortar, then pound with a pestle to combine well. The sugar will take on the red colour of the chilli powder.

For the AngloThai-style dip, mix together the lemon verbena leaves, coriander root, chillies and makrut lime zest with a pinch of the salt in a mortar, then pound with a pestle until it resembles a smooth paste. Add the remaining salt and the sugar, then pound and mix until the sugar turns a vibrant green and begins to clump slightly.

Serve with the fruit.

Both dips can be stored in airtight containers in the refrigerator for up to two weeks.

gap glaeem

miang kham

Assorted Flavour 'One-bite' Royal Snack

This snack gained favour with the Thai Royal family before finding popularity throughout the rest of Thailand. *Miang kham* literally translates as 'one-bite snack' and each leaf parcel takes your taste buds on a kaleidoscopic journey of flavours, textures and aromas. For best results, make the sauce a day or two in advance to allow the flavours to develop and mature. The raw ingredients should be cut into small pieces to ensure they work in balance and don't overpower one other. Traditionally, this snack is served on wild pepper or betel leaves, but I prefer to serve them on peppery nasturtium or large spinach leaves. Try topping the *miang kham* with picked white crab meat or caviar for a luxurious canapé at dinner parties.

SERVES 6

1 tablespoon finely diced lime (skin and flesh)
1 tablespoon finely diced ginger root
1 tablespoon finely diced red onion
2 bird's eye chillies, finely sliced
2 tablespoons grated coconut, dry-toasted in a pan until golden
1 tablespoon roasted peanuts, roughly crushed (see tip)
nasturtium leaves or large spinach leaves, to serve

For the *miang kham* sauce

1 tablespoon shrimp paste
banana leaf (optional)
1 tablespoon chopped galangal, dry-toasted in a pan until dried and fragrant
1 tablespoon dried shrimp
3 tablespoons grated coconut, dry-toasted in a pan until golden
1 tablespoon roasted peanuts (see tip)
1 teaspoon salt
310 g (11 oz/1¾ cups plus 1 teaspoon) palm or brown sugar
40 ml (1¼ fl oz/2⅔ tablespoons) water
4 tablespoons fish sauce
3 tablespoons Tamarind Water (*nahm makham piak*) (page 214)

TO GARNISH

- coriander (cilantro) leaves
- mandarin or clementine, segmented and membrane removed (optional)

To make the sauce, wrap the shrimp paste in a banana leaf or a piece of kitchen foil and dry-roast in a pan over a low heat for 2 minutes, or until fragrant, flipping once. Transfer to a mortar, along with the toasted galangal, dried shrimp, toasted coconut, roasted peanuts and salt. Pound to a smooth paste with a pestle. Alternatively, blitz in a food processor.

Warm the sugar and water together in a medium saucepan over a low heat, then simmer for 3 minutes until syrupy and thick. Add the fish sauce and pounded paste and simmer for a further 2 minutes, then add the Tamarind Water. Stir and simmer for another minute, taking care not to scorch it. Leave the sauce to cool to room temperature before tasting; it should be sweet and rich, sour and salty. Keep at room temperature. It should be the consistency of runny honey. If the sauce thickens too much as it cools, simply reheat it and allow it to return to room temperature.

In a bowl, combine the lime, ginger, red onion, chillies, toasted coconut and crushed peanuts, and dress with enough sauce to coat everything.

Serve piled on to the nasturtium leaves, garnished with coriander and segmented mandarin, if using. Alternatively, pile all the ingredients separately on a serving plate and serve with a ramekin of the sauce and the nasturtium leaves on the side, inviting your guests to build their own *miang kham* by taking a small selection of the leaf toppings and drizzling over the sauce, before wrapping and eating.

Tip: To make the roasted peanuts, preheat the oven to 180°C (350°F/gas 4). Spread the raw peanuts out over a baking tray (pan) and toast in the oven for 15 minutes, stirring frequently, until golden brown and they smell roasted and nutty. Leave to cool, then store in an airtight container for up to a month.

gap glaeem

ma hor

Hazelnut Candied Meat on Red-flesh Plum

Rather wonderfully, the Thai name *ma hor* translates to 'galloping horses' in English, which, although playful, offers very little insight into the dish's ingredients or composition. I was first introduced to *ma hor* by chef David Thompson at his Bangkok restaurant Nahm. It is an appetiser served to every guest at the restaurant, designed to invigorate the palate with its sweet, nutty, salty and fresh flavours. I've slightly tweaked the recipe taught to me at Nahm to include a few native British ingredients, like hazelnuts and plums, but the flavours remain true to chef David's version.

SERVES 6

60 g (2 oz/½ cup minus 2 teaspoons) hazelnuts
2 tablespoons chopped coriander (cilantro) root or coriander stem
2 tablespoons chopped garlic
1 teaspoon white peppercorns
1 teaspoon salt
2 tablespoons vegetable oil
180 g (6 oz/¾ cup) minced (ground) pork
100 g (3½ oz) raw prawns (shrimp), hand minced (ground)
3 tablespoons prawn (shrimp) tomalley (optional) – this is the orange coral squeezed from the prawn heads
310 g (11 oz/1¾ cups plus 1 teaspoon) palm sugar
3 tablespoons fish sauce
50 g (2 oz) Fried Shallots (*hom jiaw*) (page 210)
35 g (1¼ oz) Fried Garlic (*gratiam jiaw*) (page 211)
4 ripe red-flesh plums (or any other seasonal plum), halved, stoned (pitted) and sliced into elegant bite-size slices
1 long red chilli, seeded and finely shredded into 2.5 cm (1 in) lengths

Preheat the oven to 180°C (350°F/gas 4). Spread out the hazelnuts on a baking tray (pan) and roast for 10 minutes, stirring frequently, until they are golden brown and smell roasted and nutty. Leave to cool before adding to a pestle and mortar and pounding into a somewhat coarse texture that resembles couscous. Remove from the mortar and set aside.

Add the coriander root, garlic, white peppercorns and salt to the pestle and mortar and pound to a smooth paste.

Heat the oil in a wok over a medium heat. Add the pounded paste and stir-fry until fragrant and aromatic, making sure it doesn't colour. Add the minced pork and fry for 1 minute until cooked through. Add the minced prawns and prawn tomalley and fry for a further minute until the prawns are cooked. Reduce the heat and add the sugar and fish sauce, along with half the Fried Shallots and half the Fried Garlic. Cook, stirring constantly, for 5 minutes, or until the mixture becomes reduced and thickened.

Once sticky and reduced, remove from the heat and stir through the remaining Fried Shallots and Fried Garlic, along with the ground hazelnuts, ensuring everything is well combined. Taste: it will be sweet, rich, nutty and salty. Transfer to a container and leave to cool to room temperature. The mixture will become considerably harder, but should still be malleable. If it solidifies too much, return the mixture to a saucepan and warm with 1 tablespoon of water, then leave to cool to room temperature once more.

Roll the cooled candied meat mixture into rustic balls about the size of marbles and top each plum segment with a ball. Finish each with a few strands of shredded red chilli.

hoi naang rohm

Oysters with 'Nahm Jim' Sauce

I'm a huge fan of oysters and we usually have them on the restaurant menu: sometimes steamed and adorned with toppings; sometimes charcoal-grilled in their shells over hot coals; sometimes battered in rice flour and coconut cream, then deep-fried; but simply serving them raw with a spicy dressing has to be one of my favourite food pleasures. *Nahm jim* is a traditional Thai sauce that marries spicy, sour and salty flavours together in perfect harmony. There are many different versions of this sauce, but in this recipe I have used sea buckthorn, a native orange berry, to bring sourness and a background tropical fruit flavour. If you are unable to source sea buckthorn juice (it's usually available at health food stores or online) then use lime and orange juice, at a ratio of five parts lime juice to one part orange juice.

SERVES 6

12 live oysters, thoroughly cleaned in cold water
crushed ice, to serve (optional)

For the *nahm jim* sauce
1 long red chilli, seeded and chopped
2 red bird's eye chillies, chopped
1 tablespoon chopped coriander (cilantro) root or coriander stem
1 tablespoon chopped garlic
½ teaspoon salt
4 tablespoons sea buckthorn juice (unsweetened)
1 tablespoon lime juice
2½ tablespoons fish sauce
2 tablespoons caster (superfine) sugar

To make the *nahm jim*, pound the chillies, coriander root, garlic and salt in a pestle and mortar to a smooth paste. Add the sea buckthorn juice, lime juice, fish sauce and sugar, then mix everything together until the sugar has dissolved. Set aside for 5 minutes, allowing the flavours to mellow and marry together.

Shuck the oysters and clean them of any shell fragments. Tip away most of the oyster liquid, then spoon the *nahm jim* sauce over each oyster, using about 1 tablespoon for each. Rest the shells in a bowl of crushed ice, if using, and serve immediately.

gap glaeem

hoi chaehn pao

Roasted Scallops with Pounded Red Chilli Dressing

This simple recipe packs a punch with the bold flavours of red chilli, fish sauce and lime juice. I have suggested this as a snack, but the dish would make an impressive starter to a meal, especially with the scallop served baked in the shell. If using prepared scallops, though, they rarely come with their shells. Instead, soak bamboo skewers in water for an hour, then skewer a few scallops together and cook under a hot grill (broiler), turning once during cooking. Serve the red chilli dressing on the side as a dipping sauce or pour over just before serving.

SERVES 4

8 medium live scallops

For the red chilli dressing
1 long red chilli, seeded and chopped
2 red bird's eye chillies, chopped
1 tablespoon chopped coriander
   (cilantro) root or coriander stem
1 tablespoon chopped garlic
½ teaspoon salt
5 tablespoons lime juice
3 tablespoons fish sauce
2 tablespoons palm or brown sugar

To make the red chilli dressing, pound the chillies, coriander root, garlic and salt together in a pestle and mortar to form a smooth paste. Add the lime juice, fish sauce and sugar and mix everything together until the sugar has dissolved. Set aside for 15 minutes, allowing the flavours to mellow and marry together. It will taste spicy, sour and salty, with a background sweetness.

Clean the scallops. The best way to do this is to slide a table knife against the inside of the top (flat lid) shell, separating the scallop meat from the top shell. This will allow you to fully open the shell. Scoop the scallop out from the bottom (round bowl) shell using a tablespoon to separate the scallop meat from the bowl shell. Wash the scallop in a bowl of cold water, removing and discarding the black digestive tract. Set the white scallop meat and orange coral (roe) meat aside. Clean the round bowl shell for presentation and repeat the process until all the scallops are cleaned.

Preheat the grill (broiler) to a high heat. Cut the white scallop meat in half, leaving the orange coral whole. Return the scallops to their round bowl shells and arrange on a grill tray. Spoon 1 tablespoon of the red chilli dressing over each scallop, then grill (broil) for 1–2 minutes until just cooked through.

Remove the scallop shells from the grill and spoon another 1 tablespoon of the red chilli dressing over each scallop. Serve immediately. Be careful of the hot shells!

gap glaeem

kanom

Sweets

Thai people have an incredible love of sweet things. In my experience, *kanom* (Thai sweets) aren't necessarily reserved for after meals, but can be enjoyed throughout the day. Unsurprisingly, there are endless varieties available, ranging from rustic snacks, such as steamed sticky rice mixed with sugar and topped with toasted coconut, to highly intricate treats, such as freshly pressed and luscious rich coconut cream being infused with jasmine candle smoke before being formed into layered moulds with colourful agar jellies. There are even painstakingly made egg yolk and sugar syrup desserts that are formed into delicate and wispy threads or moulded into mock jackfruit seeds. These are influenced directly by the Portuguese egg custard confectioneries brought to Siam in the 16th century. At the other end of the spectrum, there are wonderful tropical fruits, rarely encountered in Western culture, that are attractively carved and eaten fresh at the height of their season.

pa thong ko

Dough Sticks with Pandan Custard

This recipe is based on the deep-fried bread sticks found in the food markets and street corners of Chinatown, normally cooked during the early morning or late afternoon hours. Traditionally, *pa thong ko* is simply enjoyed dipped into a bowl of sugar, although some more elaborate vendors serve these golden dough sticks with a coconut cream custard flavoured and coloured with pandan leaves. I have included measurements in metric weights for the dough sticks as this recipe requires some accuracy.

MAKES ABOUT 10 DOUGH STICKS

300 g (10½ oz/scant 2½ cups) strong white bread flour, plus extra for dusting

1½ tablespoons (22 g/¾ oz) caster (superfine) sugar

1 teaspoon (6 g/¼ oz) salt

2 teaspoons (10 g/⅓ oz) instant dried yeast

2 large eggs, beaten

4 tablespoons (60 ml/2 fl oz) whole milk

4 tablespoons (60 g/2 oz) unsalted butter, softened and diced

vegetable oil, for oiling and deep-frying

For the pandan custard
(*sangkaya dtoei hom*)

3 pandan leaves, finely chopped (or use 2 drops of pandan concentrate)

3–4 tablespoons water (optional)

1½ tablespoons rice flour

200 ml (7 fl oz/scant 1 cup) coconut cream (the richer, heavier solids that rise to the top of the thinner milk)

397 g (14 oz) can condensed milk

1 teaspoon salt

For rolling

4 tablespoons caster (superfine) sugar

½ teaspoon salt

To make the pandan custard, purée the chopped pandan leaves in a food processor with as little water as possible, about 3–4 tablespoons. Strain though a sieve (fine-mesh strainer, pressing through with a spoon to extract as much of the vivid green liquid as possible, then set aside. Mix the rice flour with a little of the coconut cream in a small bowl to make a smooth paste. Gently warm this paste with the remaining coconut cream in a medium saucepan over a low heat for 5 minutes, or until thickened, whisking constantly to ensure the mixture doesn't become lumpy. Once thickened, add the pandan juice (or concentrate), condensed milk and salt and cook, whisking constantly, for 1 minute until the custard is thick enough to coat the back of a spoon. Leave to cool to room temperature.

To make the dough, mix together the eggs and milk in a bowl and set aside. Combine all the dry ingredients in a stand mixer with a dough hook attached. While mixing at low–medium speed, gradually add the egg-and-milk mixture. It will come together into a dough. Knead the dough for about 10 minutes, or until it is very elastic, then add the butter, a few cubes at a time, until completely incorporated. This is a rich dough, so it can be very sticky to handle. Keep working the dough in the mixer until it is possible to handle.

Tip the dough out on to a clean work surface. Using your hands, bring the dough together into a smooth ball, then place in a large bowl and cover with clingfilm (plastic wrap). Leave in a warm spot for 30 minutes, or until the dough has doubled in size.

Line a baking tray (pan) with baking parchment and dust generously with flour. Tip the dough on to a clean work surface and divide into equal-size pieces of about 50 g (2 oz) each. Roll these pieces into smooth sticks about 8 cm (3¼ in) long and 2.5 cm (1 in) wide and place them on the lined tray, leaving enough space for the sticks to double in size without touching each other. Cover with oiled clingfilm and leave to prove in a warm spot for about 20 minutes, or until doubled in size.

kanom

Pour the oil for deep-frying into a large wok to a depth of 10 cm (4 in) and heat until the oil reaches 180°C (350°F) on a temperature probe. Alternatively, drop a small cube of bread into the oil; if it turns golden brown in about 15 seconds, the oil is ready.

Using a bamboo skewer, press it down the length of each dough stick to create indents that you can then use as a guide to make an 'X' shape. Working in batches, fry the X-shaped sticks for 4 minutes, or until golden brown, flipping them over halfway through to ensure both sides colour and cook evenly. Remove and drain on a plate lined with paper towels while you deep-fry the remaining dough sticks.

Combine the sugar and salt for rolling in a wide dish, then roll the still-warm dough sticks in the mixture until well coated. Serve with the pandan custard for dipping. Alternatively, instead of rolling, serve the dough sticks with the sugar mix and pandan custard in separate dishes on the side for dipping.

mamuang khao neow

Mango with Sweet Sticky Rice

This has to be the quintessential Thai dessert beloved around the world. There aren't many components to the dish, so each ingredient should be sourced well. Thailand is blessed with incredible mangoes and the yellow ones are hard to match in flavour. I personally wait until the Indian Alphonso and Kesar mango season (May–August), as they not only have a similar look to the yellow-skinned mangoes of Thailand, but, more importantly, they have the same amazing flavour. If you want to go the extra mile, then make your own coconut cream (pages 208–209) as this recipe showcases how fantastic freshly squeezed coconut cream can taste – creamy, rich and pure!

SERVES 2

150 g (5 oz/¾ cup) sticky rice (preferably from Thailand)

200 ml (7 fl oz/scant 1 cup) coconut cream (the richer, heavier solids that rise to the top of the thinner milk)

1 pandan leaf, knotted (optional, but very desirable)

120 g (4 oz/½ cup) caster (superfine) sugar

1 teaspoon salt

1 medium ripe mango, about 300 g (10½ oz)

1 teaspoon white sesame seeds, toasted

For the sweetened thick coconut cream (*gati waan*)

150 ml (5 fl oz/⅔ cup) coconut cream (the richer, heavier solids that rise to the top of the thinner milk)

1 pandan leaf, knotted (optional, but very desirable)

1½ tablespoons caster (superfine) sugar

¼ teaspoon salt

½ teaspoon rice flour

To make the sweetened thick coconut cream, put the coconut milk, pandan leaf (if using), sugar and salt into a large saucepan. Warm over a low heat for 5 minutes, stirring constantly, until the sugar has dissolved. Mix the rice flour and a little of the warm coconut cream together in a small bowl until a smooth paste forms, then stir this mixture back into the pan of sweet coconut cream. Warm for another minute, stirring constantly, until the sweet coconut cream becomes thick enough to coat the back of a spoon. Leave to cool to room temperature.

Steam the sticky rice (see instructions on page 196). Meanwhile, put the coconut milk, pandan leaf, if using, sugar and salt into another saucepan and warm over a low heat for 5 minutes, stirring constantly, until the sugar has dissolved. The coconut cream will taste excessively sweet, but it needs to be in order to properly season the cooked sticky rice.

Once the sticky rice is cooked, transfer to a plastic container and pour over the second batch of prepared coconut cream. Mix well to completely incorporate the coconut cream mixture with the rice grains. It's important the rice is hot as this will allow the grains to fully absorb the liquid and become attractively glistening. Cover the surface of the sticky rice with clingfilm (plastic wrap), then cover the container with a lid. Leave to stand in a warm place for 10 minutes to allow the cream to be fully absorbed and the rice to rest.

Peel the mango with a sharp knife, then cut away the two lobes from the central stone. Cut each lobe widthways into 2.5 cm (1 in) slices.

Stir the sticky rice to loosen the grains, then divide between two shallow bowls. Place the sliced mango alongside the sticky rice, then cover the mango and sticky rice with a few tablespoons of the cooled sweetened thick coconut cream. Serve sprinkled with the toasted sesame seeds.

ice cream khao hom mali

Jasmine Rice Ice Cream

All flavours and colours of ice cream are eaten throughout Thailand, ranging from the more orthodox coconut ice cream to the fairly unusual durian fruit – a complex-flavoured fruit that has sweet, savoury and creamy notes, and is unlike anything else I have ever tried. I like this recipe as it showcases the aromatic and almost floral flavour of the jasmine rice, in an equally sweet and savoury ice cream. The additional jasmine rice crackers give a lovely texture contrast with the soft ice cream.

SERVES 10

500 ml (17 fl oz/2 cups) whole milk
750 ml (25 fl oz/3 cups) double (heavy) cream
350 g (12 oz/1¾ cups) jasmine rice (preferably Thai)
397 g (14 oz) can condensed milk
500 ml (17 fl oz/2 cups) water
2 tablespoons caster (superfine) sugar
1 teaspoon salt
vegetable oil, for deep-frying
3 tablespoons icing (confectioners') sugar
150 g (5 oz/⅔ cup) sweet fermented rice (*khao mak*), optional

To make the ice cream, place the whole milk and cream in a large saucepan over a medium heat and bring to a simmer. Add the jasmine rice to a bowl and pour the warm milk and cream mixture over the rice grains. Cover and leave to infuse overnight in the refrigerator (for at least 10 hours).

The next day, strain the mixture through a sieve (fine-mesh strainer) and set the rice aside for later. Add the condensed milk to the liquid mixture and combine well, then churn in an ice-cream maker, following the manufacturer's instructions. Transfer the ice cream to the freezer until ready to serve.

To make the jasmine rice crackers, line a baking tray (pan) with baking parchment. Add the water to a large saucepan, along with 5 oz (¾ cup) of the strained jasmine rice. Bring to the boil and cook for 25 minutes, or until completely overcooked and very soft. Transfer to a food processor, along with the caster sugar and salt, and blitz until completely smooth. Spread the resulting rice paste out on to the lined baking trays to an even 2 mm (1/16 in) thickness. Place the trays in a dehydrator or low oven set to 55°C (131°F/lowest possible gas) for 6 hours, or until you have brittle crackers.

Pour the oil for deep-frying into a large wok to a depth of 10 cm (4 in) and heat until the oil reaches 190°C (375°F) on a cooking thermometer. Alternatively, drop a small cube of bread into the hot oil; if it turns golden brown in about 10 seconds, the oil is ready. Break the dried jasmine rice crackers into 8 cm (3 in) pieces and deep-fry in batches for 15 seconds, until puffed out. Drain well on paper towels, then sprinkle with a light dusting of icing sugar.

Serve a spoonful of the jasmine rice ice cream per person, spoon over 1 tablespoon of the sweet fermented rice and top with the rice crackers.

Note on sweet fermented rice (*khao mak*): Sweet fermented rice is available in Asian supermarkets, usually in glass jars with red lids. It is also known as Chinese fermented rice dessert. The process involves fermenting sticky rice with yeast balls and sugar for several weeks. The result is a broken-down rice grain with a slightly alcoholic (around 1% ABV) and sweet liquor. *Khao mak* has a pleasant alcohol flavour with a not overly sweet taste, and is often eaten chilled in this form by Thai people.

som choon

Fig Leaf Syrup Iced Fruits

Som choon is a sweet and refreshing dessert usually made during rambutan and lychee season to showcase these wonderful sweet and sour fruits. The fruits are steeped in an aromatic syrup perfumed with pandan leaf and citrus juice, then served chilled over shaved ice with shredded green mango. I have made many incarnations of this dish over the years, but this recipe is one of my favourites, employing the principles of a traditional *som choon* but using British ingredients. Fig trees grow abundantly, so keep an eye out for them, as a few picked leaves will go a long way when making infused sugar syrups like this one. I find the leaves have a sweet, almost coconutty aroma and flavour that makes them perfect for Thai desserts. If fig leaves aren't available, then omit them, as this recipe will still produce a lovely flavoured syrup for the fruits.

SERVES 8

1 litre (34 fl oz/4 cups) water
3 tablespoons pandan juice (page 180) or ½ teaspoon pandan concentrate
315 g (11 oz/1⅓ cups) caster (superfine) sugar
¼ teaspoon salt
1 piece of dried mandarin peel (page 34)
zest of 1 makrut or regular lime
1 pandan leaf, knotted
100 g (3½ oz) fig leaves
juice of ½ mandarin
juice of ½ lime
565 g (20 oz) can lychees in syrup, drained
200 g (7 oz/2 cups) strawberries, halved or quartered, depending on their size
100 g (3½ oz) forced pink rhubarb, finely shredded or green apple such as Granny Smith

Mix 500 ml (17 fl oz/2 cups) of the water with the pandan juice and 1 tablespoon of the sugar in a large bowl until the sugar has dissolved and the water is a vivid green colour. You may need to add more pandan juice to achieve the right colour depending on how strong it is. Pour into a plastic container and freeze overnight.

The next day, combine the remaining 500 ml (17 fl oz/2 cups) water with the remaining sugar in a large saucepan and gently simmer over a low heat for 5 minutes to create a sugar syrup. Once the sugar has completely dissolved, simmer for another 2 minutes, then remove from the heat and add the salt, dried mandarin peel, makrut lime zest, pandan leaf and fig leaves. Set aside to infuse for at least 5 hours. Once the syrup is infused and has cooled to room temperature, season with the mandarin and lime juices. It should taste sweet and aromatic with a background salty-sourness.

Turn out the frozen pandan ice and carefully break it up using a stone pestle and mortar; you are looking for a crushed ice texture. Divide the ice, lychees and strawberries between individual serving bowls and top with a few tablespoons of the infused syrup. Scatter over the shredded rhubarb or apple, then serve.

ngaai

Basics

This chapter covers items that I refer to as 'basics', but perhaps they should be referred to as essentials for cooking dishes from this book. I have started the chapter with one of the most important – if not *the* most important – food items in the Thai repertoire: rice. This section gives you some background about the two main types of rice consumed in Thailand and how to cook each of them. It might be said that mastering the skill of rice cookery is more important than any other technique or recipe in this book, considering all other dishes are designed to be eaten with rice. Other recipes in this chapter focus on pantry staples that are used throughout the book. These range from stocks and chilli powder to relishes and dips, the latter two being some of the most ancient dishes in the Thai culinary repertoire, as the ingredients used and the techniques employed date back to the earliest recordings of Thai cookery. This is far from an exhaustive list of basics in Thai cookery, but it should go some way towards giving you a range of different items that will help you create amazing quality Thai food at home.

khao
Rice

It wouldn't be an overstatement to say that without rice, there is no Thai cuisine. Rice is a massively important and sacred food source for Thai people, deeply ingrained in Thai culture, religion and traditions. To serve a meal without rice would be completely unthinkable. In early Thai history, rice would have been the centrepiece of a meal, perhaps supplemented with an intensely pungent chilli paste (*nahm prik*) to add flavour and seasoning, alongside a plate of local or foraged vegetables, and, if you were lucky, some meat or fish. As the centuries rolled on and middle-class status rose in Thailand, so did the ability and want for more elaborate dishes to accompany rice. Nowadays, Thai people indulge more in meats, fats and other more expensive food items, but in keeping with their ancestors, rice remains the focal point of the meal. Over the centuries, Thai cooks have designed and created dishes with the assumption that they would be eaten alongside rice. This goes some way towards explaining why dishes in the Thai culinary repertoire are so strongly flavoured: they are intended to accompany and season relatively bland rice. This same assumption should be considered today when eating Thai food, and explains why eating a pungent curry or stir-fry without rice would be misguided. It could be compared to eating spaghetti Bolognese, but without the spaghetti – I think you'll agree, quite absurd behaviour. Thai dishes need rice to mellow their intense flavours, and at the same time rely on these big flavours to season the rice grains themselves. That is not to say that rice holds no flavour: its subtle nuttiness and perfumed fragrance not only complement but complete many Thai dishes. Rice is the yin to the yang for a balanced Thai meal.

khao hom mali
Steamed Jasmine Rice

Not all jasmine rice grains are created equal. At markets in Thailand, you will see rice vendors with various bins of raw rice grains from different provinces, rice crops and ages, just as you would expect to see a cheesemonger in Britain displaying all his different cheeses. The various rice grains command different prices depending on how prized they are, with the most expensive being new-crop rice, which are grains sold shortly after being harvested, when the water content is at its highest and the rice is at its most fragrant. Overseas, we only really have access to new-crop rice that has been aged for a year or so in bags; it has a lower water content that makes it easier and more consistent to steam. There is nothing wrong with this rice, as the grains still hold a lovely fragrance. I do recommend looking for rice grown in Thailand, as this holds the best fragrance and complements the dishes in this book best.

As mentioned on page 40, I recommend investing in an electric rice cooker as it makes your life easier and is an indispensable piece of kit for anyone cooking Thai food regularly. If you are, however, opposed to the idea of buying a rice cooker, or you're still making your mind up on it, then I've included methods for both using an electric rice cooker and a saucepan with lid on the hob. For these 'absorption method' recipes, I use a cup measurement as I find volume is better than weight in this instance. As a rule, I account for a standard cup of rice for two people, therefore these instructions make enough for four people.

SERVES 4–6

400 g (14 oz/2 cups) long-grain jasmine rice (preferably from Thailand)
600 ml (20 fl oz/2½ cups) water

ELECTRIC RICE COOKER METHOD

In a large bowl, rinse the rice under cold running water, stirring the rice with the water. The water will become very cloudy as excess starch leaches from the rice grains. Pour off this cloudy water and repeat the process twice more. Drain the rice well in a sieve (fine-mesh strainer).

Transfer the rinsed and drained rice to the rice cooker and spread the rice out into an even layer, then pour over the measured water to cover. If you want to follow a traditional method of how much water to use, hold your index finger vertically in the water so the tip of your finger touches the surface of the rice. The level of the water should be level with the first knuckle of your index finger – this is the way my grandmother and mother taught me to cook rice originally, and I still use this method today.

Close the lid and press the button to steam, usually labelled 'cook'.

When the rice is done steaming, leave to stand, covered, for 5–10 minutes so that the residual steam inside the cooker is absorbed back into the rice, making the grains plump and tender. After the rice has rested, open the rice cooker and fluff the rice from the bottom up using the plastic spoon that comes as standard with all electric rice cookers. The aim is to separate the individual rice grains without crushing or breaking them. If your rice cooker has a 'keep warm' setting (which almost all do) then you can switch to this setting to keep the rice warm and fluffy for a few hours if you're not planning to serve it immediately.

SAUCEPAN AND LID METHOD

Rinse and drain the rice as described opposite.

Transfer the rinsed and drained rice to a medium saucepan with a tight-fitting lid and cover with the measured water, or use the finger method described opposite.

Bring the water and rice to a fast boil, uncovered, over a high heat. Once at boiling point, stir the rice, cover with the lid and reduce the heat to the lowest heat setting on your hob. Simmer for 12–15 minutes, trying not to lift the lid until 12 minutes have passed, as the escaping steam will cause the rice to cook unevenly. After 12 minutes, check the rice; there should be no visible water left in the pan and the rice grains should be tender but still retain their individual structure. If the rice is hard or there is water visible, then keep cooking with the lid on for another few minutes.

Remove the pan from the heat and leave the rice to stand, covered, for 5–10 minutes so that the residual steam inside the pan is absorbed back into the rice, making the grains plump and tender. After the rice has rested, uncover and fluff the rice from the bottom up using a spoon or fork. The aim is to separate the individual rice grains without crushing or breaking them. Serve immediately.

khao neow

Sticky Rice

Sticky rice is the favoured starch of Northern and neighbouring Northeastern Thailand or Isaan. The rice grains require soaking for several hours before steaming, so traditionally this is the last chore in a Thai household before going to bed. I romantically think about it as putting the sticky rice to bed before heading off for some shut-eye myself. As the rice soaks, it absorbs the water and swells. It might sound obvious, but be sure to cover the rice with enough water so that it doesn't become bone dry by the time you come to cook it. Generally speaking, I wouldn't recommend soaking the rice for longer than 12 hours, as then it has a tendency to turn into mush as it steams from over-saturation. In Thai households, sticky rice is steamed in woven bamboo baskets set over large conical shaped pots, where the swollen grains cook in about 20 minutes. You can replicate this at home using a conventional shaped metal or bamboo steamer, but if you did want to buy a sticky rice steamer set, they are readily available online. I admit there is something particularly comforting about the fragrant smell of rice steaming in bamboo drifting through the house as it cooks. I add a knotted pandan leaf to the simmering water to give extra fragrance, but this is not essential.

SERVES 4–6

400 g (14 oz/2 cups) sticky rice
  (preferably from Thailand)
1 pandan leaf, knotted (optional)

Add the sticky rice to a large bowl or container and cover with plenty of cold water, giving the rice a mix so the water envelops each grain. I allow for at least 5 cm (2 in) of water to sit above the level of the rice. Leave the rice to soak for at least 5 hours, but overnight is better.

Strain the soaked rice, then transfer to a large bowl. Rinse the rice under cold running water, stirring the rice with the water. The water will become very cloudy as excess starch leaches from the rice grains. Pour off the cloudy water and repeat this process twice more. Drain the rice well in a sieve (fine-mesh strainer).

Pour water into a steamer pot to a depth of 5 cm (2 in) and bring to the boil over a high heat. At this point, add the pandan leaf to the water, if using. Reduce the heat to maintain a steady simmer.

Transfer the soaked sticky rice to the perforated steamer and shape into a rough mound. Surprisingly few grains will fall through the holes of the steamer, so don't be tempted to set the rice on a plate or other surface that will prevent the steam from properly permeating the rice, thus inefficiently cooking the grains. Place the steamer over the boiling water and steam the rice for 25 minutes until the grains are fully tender but slightly chewy. The mound of rice requires flipping over halfway through the steaming process with a vegetable steamer. Tease apart the mound of rice and check if the middle grains are fully tender, as this shows the rice is completely cooked.

Remove from the steamer and transfer to a large bowl. Cover with a plate and leave the rice to rest for 10 minutes in a warm place before serving. It will stay warm in this covered state for up to an hour.

nahm cheua
Stock

Stock is not just a cooking staple in Thailand; it features in all cuisines I have explored. Stocks are used as a starting block for flavour, creating depth, roundedness and concentration that affects the final taste of a dish. In my experience, having a good stock to hand can not only transform a dish, but can also be used as a dish in its own right, as is commonplace in Thailand. At times, a simple bone broth is served alongside a wider meal, perhaps with a few bones to gnaw on and some chunks of simmered vegetables. They are to be sipped and savoured throughout a meal, soothing the palate and bringing respite. These almost neutral stocks, broths and soups are used to balance the pungent and intensely seasoned dishes that are plentiful throughout Thai cuisine. Thai stocks tend to be lighter, simpler and less assertive than those made in Western kitchens. Rarely are bones roasted before simmering; instead, cooks favour blanching from a cold start to remove impurities, giving a clear stock with bright clarity of flavour. I see the benefits of both Thai and Western-style stocks, and have magpied elements from both cultures for those I cook with at home and at the restaurant. The first time you make these stocks, I recommend following the recipes so you can understand the nuances of how each aromatic ingredient plays off and supports the others. This will then allow you to create your own stocks based on what you have at hand, often utilising scraps and trimmings of different ingredients so as to not waste anything in your kitchen.

nahm cheua jay
Vegetable Stock

I prefer my vegetable stock to be light with a subtle, yet true vegetable flavour, so it can be used across a diverse range of dishes. It's best made and used on the same day, but can be made in larger batches and frozen in portions for convenience. You will notice this recipe is rather vague, showing the flexibility to use what's on hand to create a lovely perfumed stock.

MAKES 2–3 LITRES (70–100 FL OZ/8–12 CUPS)

2 tough outer leaves of a cabbage
1 white onion, quartered
3 spring onions (scallions) or, better yet, the otherwise discarded roots, tops and outer skins of the spring onions, as they still hold abundant flavour
1 medium carrot, chopped, or equivalent weight of white radish/daikon
2 celery stalks, chopped
3 tablespoons mushroom stalks
3 tablespoons coriander (cilantro) stems
1½ tablespoons garlic cloves, bruised
5 cm (2 in) piece of ginger root, peeled and sliced
1 pandan leaf, knotted (optional)
¼ teaspoon white peppercorns

Place all the ingredients in a stockpot. Cover with enough water to sit 5 cm (2 in) above the vegetables, then bring to the boil over a high heat. Once it's boiling, reduce the heat to low and simmer for 2 hours. You want the water to be blipping gently, with small bubbles breaking on the surface of the stock; any stronger and the heat will be too violent.

Pass the stock through a sieve (fine-mesh strainer), discarding the vegetables and aromatics. Leave to cool completely before storing in an airtight container in the refrigerator for up to three days, or freeze in portions for up to six months.

nahm cheua gai

Chicken Stock

This is an example of blending Asian and Western-style stocks, resulting in a light but vibrantly flavoured chicken stock. I favour roasting the bones over cold blanching, as I feel the flavour of chicken is subtle enough to not become overpowering if given a darker, richer flavour from the roasting process. Unlike with chicken stocks made in Western culture, I don't roast the vegetables, and I add ginger, lemongrass and coriander (cilantro) to give an overarching lightness to the finished stock.

MAKES 2–3 LITRES (70–100 FL OZ/8–12 CUPS)

1.5 kg (3 lb 5 oz) chicken bones
500 g (1lb 2 oz) chicken wings (if you prefer, you can use just chicken bones, but increase the weight to 2 kg/4 lb 8 oz)
1 white onion, quartered
3 spring onions (scallions) or, better yet, the otherwise discarded roots, tops and outer skins of the spring onions, as they still hold abundant flavour
4 tablespoons coriander (cilantro) stems
2 tablespoons garlic cloves, bruised
8 cm (3 in) piece of ginger root, peeled and sliced
1 lemongrass stalk, chopped and bruised, or, better yet, the otherwise discarded roots, tops and outer husks of lemongrass stalks as they still hold abundant flavour
1 pandan leaf, knotted (optional)
½ teaspoon white peppercorns

Preheat the oven to 200°C (400°F/gas 7). Wash the chicken bones and wings under cold running water and drain well. Using a cleaver or heavy knife, chop the bones into large pieces of about 10 cm (4 in), but leave the chicken wings whole. Place on a baking tray (pan) and roast for 25 minutes until the bones are golden brown and crispy. There may be some rendered chicken fat produced during the roasting, so drain this off and keep for another use. Do not add the rendered fat to your stock as it will cause the final stock to become cloudy.

Transfer the roasted bones and wings to a stockpot with the remaining ingredients. Cover with enough water to sit 5 cm (2 in) above the bones and vegetables, then bring to the boil over a high heat. Once it's boiling, reduce the heat to low and simmer for 2 hours. You want the water to be blipping gently, with small bubbles breaking on the surface of the stock; any stronger and the heat will be too violent.

Pass the stock through a sieve (fine-mesh strainer), discarding the chicken bones, vegetables and aromatics. Leave the stock to cool completely, and if you wish, skim the fat and impurities off the surface of the stock as it cools. Store in the refrigerator for up to three days, or freeze in portions for up to six months.

Note: If you're anything like me, then reserve the soft braised chicken wings after straining the stock. Leave them to steam out and cool slightly before roasting in a preheated hot oven at 220°C (425°F/gas 7) for 5 minutes, so they become very crispy and golden. Alternatively, deep-fry in hot oil (about 180°C/350°F) for 2–3 minutes until golden. Season with salt and Toasted Chilli Powder (page 213), then snack on the crispy wings with an ice-cold beer!

nahm cheua mu

Pork Stock

This is the preferred stock in Northern and Northeastern Thailand due to the amount of pork consumed in those parts of the country. I like to use pork ribs as the simmered bones can be served in a lightly seasoned bone broth as a side dish or light meal in its own right, ensuring nothing goes to waste. If you have other pork bones available to you, then this recipe will produce the same results, and it's infinitely better to use what you have to hand than to buy additional bones. If you want to give your pork stock an unctuous body, then add a chopped pork trotter (foot) in with the ribs or bones.

MAKES 2–3 LITRES (70–100 FL OZ/8–12 CUPS)

2 kg (4 lb 8 oz) pork ribs, chopped into 8 cm (3 in) pieces (or pork bones)
1 white onion, quartered
3 spring onions (scallions) or, better yet, the otherwise discarded roots, tops and outer skins of the spring onions, as they still hold abundant flavour
1 medium carrot, chopped or equivalent weight of white radish/daikon
4 tablespoons coriander (cilantro) stems
2 tablespoons garlic cloves, bruised
8 cm (3 in) piece of ginger root, peeled and sliced
1 lemongrass stalk, chopped and bruised, or, better yet, the otherwise discarded roots, tops and outer husks of lemongrass stalks, as they still hold abundant flavour
1 pandan leaf, knotted (optional)
½ teaspoon white peppercorns

Wash the pork ribs or bones under cold running water. Add them to a stockpot and cover with enough water to sit 3 cm (1¼ in) above the bones, then bring to a simmer over a high heat. Once at a simmer, turn off the heat, drain the pork bones and rinse them well under cold running water. This cold-blanching process will remove blood and impurities from the bones, giving you a cleaner-tasting and -looking final stock. Clean your stockpot well, removing any scum from the base and sides.

Return the blanched bones to the stockpot and cover with enough water to sit 5 cm (2 in) above the bones. Bring to the boil over a high heat. Once it's boiling, reduce the heat to low and simmer for 2 hours. You want the water to be blipping gently, with small bubbles breaking on the surface of the stock; any stronger and the heat will be too violent.

After 2 hours, add the remaining ingredients and simmer for another 1½ hours.

Pass the stock through a sieve (fine-mesh strainer), discarding the vegetables, aromatics and bones, but setting aside the pork ribs for another use (see note). Leave the stock to cool completely, and if you wish, skim the fat and impurities off the surface of the stock as it cools. Store in the refrigerator for up to three days, or freeze in portions for up to six months.

Note: Warm a few ladlefuls of the pork stock gently with the reserved pork ribs in a large saucepan for 3–5 minutes, then season the broth lightly with a dash of fish sauce and a pinch of sugar and ground white pepper. Finish with some thinly shredded ginger root, a few sliced spring onions (scallions) and coriander (cilantro) leaves. Serve with jasmine rice as a light meal, or enjoy as a simple style soup (*gaeng jeut sii krong mu*) as part of a wider Thai meal.

nahm cheua neua

Beef Stock

For me, beef bones produce the daddy of all stocks, but it should be used with consideration, as its bigger, deeper flavour can change a dish dramatically. For example, I wouldn't use this robust stock as the base of a hot and sour soup (*dtom yum*) or a sour orange curry (*gaeng som*) as the flavour of the beef stock would fight against the fragrant aromatics that should take centre stage. Beef stock would, however, match well with a dish such as Peanut-enriched Curry of Beef Cheek and Thai Basil (*gaeng panang neua*) (page 148), where the main protein is already beef, and the flavours of the dish are bold enough to be supported by the rich stock.

MAKES 2–3 LITRES (70–100 FL OZ/8–12 CUPS)

2 kg (4 lb 8 oz) beef bones, cut into pieces that will fit in your stockpot

2 white onions, quartered

1 medium carrot, chopped, or equivalent weight of white radish/daikon

3 tablespoons mushroom stalks or a few dried shiitake mushrooms

4 tablespoons coriander (cilantro) stems

3 tablespoons garlic cloves, bruised

8 cm (3 in) piece of ginger root, peeled and sliced

2 lemongrass stalks, chopped and bruised, or, better yet, the otherwise discarded roots, tops and outer husks of lemongrass stalks as they still hold abundant flavour

½ teaspoon black peppercorns

Preheat the oven to 200°C (400°F/gas 7). Wash the beef bones under cold running water and drain well. Place on a baking tray (pan) and transfer to the oven for 20 minutes until the bones are golden brown and crispy. There may be some rendered beef fat produced during the roasting, so drain this off and keep for another use. Do not add the rendered fat to your stock, as it will cause the final stock to become cloudy.

Transfer the roasted bones to a stockpot and cover with enough water to sit 5 cm (2 in) above the bones. Bring to the boil over a high heat. Once it's boiling, reduce the heat to low and simmer for 2 hours. You want the water to be blipping gently, with small bubbles breaking on the surface of the stock; any stronger and the heat will be too violent.

After 2 hours, add the remaining ingredients and simmer for another 2 hours.

Pass the stock through a sieve (fine-mesh strainer), discarding the beef bones, vegetables and aromatics. Return the strained stock to a clean stockpot, bring back to a rapid boil, then lower the heat and simmer for 1 hour to reduce the volume by one-quarter. This will intensify the flavour of the stock, giving it a point of difference from your chicken and pork stocks. remove from the heat and leave to cool completely. If you wish, skim the fat and impurities off the surface of the stock as it cools. Store in the refrigerator for up to three days, or freeze in portions for up to six months.

Note: If you like to gnaw on crispy roasted beef bones like I do, then follow the steps in the footnote for chicken stock (page 200). The method above can also be used for making stock with venison and veal bones.

nahm cheua pla

Fish Stock

When it comes to fish stock, I aim for a light, fresh-tasting and fragrant broth that's perfumed with aromatic ingredients like coriander (cilantro), ginger and lemongrass. Thai basil stalks give a subtle anise flavour that is comparable to the use of fennel and dill in traditional fish *fumet* of European kitchens. It is important to mention you should only use bones from white fish, such as cod, hake, sea bass and flat fish (turbot, brill, sole). The fish bones must be cleaned of blood and gills removed, as these impart a bitter taste and cloud the final stock. The heads of fish add bags of flavour and contain natural gelatine, which will give the stock body. Bones and heads of oily fish, like salmon, mackerel and tuna, are too fatty and will make the stock greasy and unpleasant. If I find myself with surplus bones from these oily fish, I smoke them for prolonged periods over coconut husks and charcoal, so they lose their oiliness and instead are impregnated with the flavour of the smoke. These bones can then be used to infuse into stocks, similar to *pla krob* – an ancient Thai preserved ingredient made from coconut smoked and dried fish.

MAKES 2 LITRES (70 FL OZ/8 CUPS)

1.5 kg (3 lb 5 oz) white fish bones
500 g (1 lb 2 oz) fish heads, gills and eyes removed
1 sheet of kombu (seaweed)
1 white onion, quartered
3 spring onions (scallions) or, better yet, the otherwise discarded roots, tops and outer skins of the spring onions, as they still hold abundant flavour
1 celery stalk, chopped
4 tablespoons coriander (cilantro) stems
2 tablespoons garlic cloves, bruised
8 cm (3 in) piece of ginger root, peeled and sliced
2 lemongrass stalks, chopped and bruised, or, better yet, the otherwise discarded roots, tops and outer husks of lemongrass stalks, as they still hold abundant flavour
6 tablespoons Thai basil stalks
1 pandan leaf, knotted (optional)
½ teaspoon white peppercorns

Wash the fish bones and heads under cold running water, scrapping at any bloodlines to remove the blood. Add them to a stockpot and cover with enough water to sit 3 cm (1¼ in) above the bones. Quickly bring to a simmer over a high heat, then turn off the heat and carefully drain the bones, rinsing them well under cold running water. Clean your stockpot well, removing any scum from the base and sides.

Transfer the bones to the stockpot with the remaining ingredients. Cover with enough water to sit 5 cm (2 in) above the bones and vegetables and bring to the boil over a high heat. Once it's boiling, reduce the heat to low and simmer for 30 minutes. You want the water to be blipping gently, with small bubbles breaking on the surface of the stock; any stronger, and the heat will be too violent. If necessary, skim the surface of any impurities.

Remove from the heat, cover the pan with a lid and leave for 1 hour for the flavours to infuse. During this time, the bones and other ingredients will fall to the base of the stockpot.

Using a ladle, carefully scoop out the fish stock and pass it through a sieve (fine-mesh strainer) lined with muslin (cheesecloth). Try not to agitate and move the fish bones that have settled at the base of the pot, as this will cloud your stock. Ladle and strain as much of the stock as you can before you start to unsettle the bones, then discard the remainder of the stock, fish bones and other ingredients. Leave the stock to cool completely. Store in the refrigerator for up to three days, or freeze in portions for up to six months.

khreuang gaeng

Curry Paste

This section doesn't give a specific recipe, but instead provides information on the different ingredients, styles and techniques of Thai curry pastes. There is no wrong or right method of making curry paste, so please feel free to use this section as a guide and adapt the methods and information as you deem fit given your own circumstances and kitchen equipment. If you don't feel comfortable buying all the required ingredients or equipment to make your own curry paste at home, then that is also fine. I would rather readers buy a shop-bought curry paste (see page 33 for recommended curry paste brands) and give the recipes in this book a try rather than omit them completely. Quite frankly, life is too short to miss out on trying new things because someone told you to do it a certain way.

Even if you know next to nothing about Thai food, I would bet that, at a minimum, most readers associate curry with the cuisine, in particular green curry (*gaeng kheo wan*) and red curry (*gaeng ped*), which are the most widely known curries outside of Thailand. It's no surprise that these styles of curries have gained fame worldwide. This is mainly due to their deliciously rich, warming and complex properties. But to stop at these curries would be a travesty, as the varieties available throughout the Thai kingdom are vast and colourful. Ingredients vary due to location and season, and cooks implement widely different techniques to reflect personal tastes. This results in hundreds of varieties of curry pastes that have been developed and refined over the centuries of Thai food history.

On the whole, most modern-day curry pastes involve the same basic aromatic fresh ingredients and spices: chillies (dried or fresh), shallots, garlic, coriander (cilantro) root, galangal and shrimp paste, with the proportions of each ingredient adjusted to highlight the nuances of certain flavour profiles. Each ingredient should be detectable in the final paste, with no one flavour overpowering the others; the ingredients should meld together as a whole, working in balance and harmony, with each one enhancing the other flavours in the final

curry. The sheer volume of robust flavours that are married together in harmony is a marvel of Thai cuisine, and is something I find fascinating. Other common ingredients found in curry pastes include makrut lime zest, turmeric root, fingerroot, roasted coconut, dried spices and peanuts.

When preparing a curry paste, it's vital that fresh ingredients are cleaned, peeled and finely chopped, as this will result in less work when pounding the final paste. As a rule, the hardest, most fibrous ingredients with less water content are added to the mortar first, and these should be pounded into a smooth paste before incorporating the next ingredient. As you incorporate softer ingredients with more water content, the paste will become more wet and slippery in the mortar, making it increasingly difficult to incorporate the ingredient with the others. When preparing to pound a curry paste, ensure that you place the mortar on a folded tea (dish) towel to reduce its movement. If working on a table or bench, then position the mortar over a corner or table leg to blunt the impact of the pestle pounding into the mortar. Hold the pestle firmly but with a loose wrist, and as you pound, let the weight of the pestle do the hard work for you – gravity will take care of the rest. When you drop your pestle into the mortar, aim for where the top of the ingredients meet the mortar. Make a clean connection and allow the pestle and ingredients to slide down the wall towards the very base of the mortar bowl. Repeating this action will create friction and abrasion, breaking open the fibres and cell structures of the ingredients, and ultimately allowing them to meld together. It's useful to have a spoon on hand to scoop and scrape the paste off the sides of the mortar to ensure everything is well crushed and combined together. If you choose to make fresh curry pastes using this traditional method, then be sure to add the ingredients to the mortar in the order given in the recipe, as this dictates the easiest order to successfully achieve a smooth paste that is rich in aroma and fully rounded in flavour.

Chillies dictate a number of factors in a curry

paste, including the colour and spice level. Dried chillies are the most commonly used when making curry paste, as they are large, fleshy and milder than their fiercely intense bird's eye chilli counterparts. When preparing the long dried chillies, remove the stem and break open the pods to remove any seeds and membranes, which are where the majority of the chillies' heat lies; some prefer to wear gloves for this. Soak the chilli flesh in cold water for 12–15 minutes. This same process is used for dried bird's eye chillies, but the seeds are rarely removed. This soaking will not only rehydrate the chillies for use, but will also ensure some of the chilli heat is leached, resulting in a fuller, richer chilli flavour – plus, it means you are able to use more chillies for an attractive depth of colour. Soaked chillies must be squeezed of all excess water in order to not dilute the final curry paste; this will also make it easier to fully purée in the mortar. If fresh long chillies are called for in a recipe, simply remove the stem, split the chilli and discard the seeds and white fleshy membrane. A final note when using chillies in curry pastes; add them to the mortar first, and with a large pinch of salt: not only will this add seasoning to the paste from the beginning, but it will also cause abrasion to help crush and very finely chop the chillies. For recipes in this book, ½ teaspoon of salt will be enough to achieve this, ensuring the final paste is fuller and rounded in flavour as opposed to hollow and under-seasoned.

Dried spices hold an important role in a number of curry pastes, but generally speaking, those pastes with foreign heritage, such as the Muslim-influenced *gaeng massaman* and Burmese spiced *gaeng hung lae*, are the ones that commonly call for these spices. Dried spices are used to add another dimension and piquancy to the fresh aromatic ingredients used. With the exception of peppercorns, all dried spices should be toasted prior to being ground and added to pastes. Dried spices are added last to a curry paste. Prior to their addition, the paste should be vibrantly fragrant and aromatic; afterwards, it will become earthier and rich, with a deeper complexity. I would always recommend adding two-thirds the volume of ground spices to your curry paste before gradually working in the rest, using your intuition and senses to know when to stop. It is imperative not to overly spice the curry paste, as a paste that is too heavy in dry spices will not create a traditional Thai curry but something more relatable to Indian cookery. Dried spices that are commonly used in pastes include white peppercorns (and sometimes black or long peppercorns), coriander seeds, cumin seeds, cassia bark, cloves and nutmeg.

If you don't use all the curry paste in a recipe, then it can be happily stored in the refrigerator for up to two weeks. Ensure it is in an airtight container with a layer of baking parchment or clingfilm (plastic wrap) touching the surface to stop oxidation and discoloration. If you do decide to freeze the curry paste, this is fine, but be aware that when thawed, it will lack its original vibrancy of flavour and can sometimes turn bitter.

hua gati

Fresh Coconut Cream

At the restaurant, we make fresh coconut cream daily for use in a variety of dishes. The applications are endless, from coconut-based curries and soups, to braising meats and vegetables, enriching dressings, creating elegant simmered relishes or flavouring sweets. The taste of freshly made coconut cream is something that can only be described as lusciously delicious, with a deep complexity and rich creaminess. If you want to try making your own fresh coconut cream, then you will need to source some older brown coconuts (the sort you see at the fairground coconut shy). When selecting brown coconuts, opt for a heavy nut for its size, meaning there will be more flesh and therefore a greater yield. It's also worth noting that if you feel water in the nut when shaken, then this is a good sign, as the flesh is less likely to be fermented or, worse yet, rancid. Two regular coconuts will yield around 400 ml (13 fl oz/generous 1½ cups) of fresh cream. You will also need a food processor and a heavy dull object, such as a granite pestle, the back of a cleaver, or even a hammer.

Using a folded tea (dish) towel, hold the coconut firmly with your less dominant hand over a sink or bowl. Give the coconut husk a measured but firm knock with your dull object in order to crack the husk. Repeat this process across the equator of the coconut until it splits open.

Prise the coconut flesh from the husk using a blunt knife (I like to use an oyster shuck to do this), while trying to keep the coconut flesh in pieces as large as possible.

If you want to make bright white coconut cream, you will need to peel the thin brown skin off the back of the coconut where the flesh was touching the husk. If you're not worried about this, then skipping this step will save time, but will result in an off-white coloured cream. In general, I don't worry about peeling the flesh unless I'm planning to show off the colour of the cream in the finished dish or garnish, such as in Mango with Sweet Sticky Rice (*mamuang khao neuw*) (page 184), but if this is just going to be added to a vibrant curry paste, then the whiteness of your cream will be insignificant.

Wash the coconut flesh in plenty of clean cold water and drain well using a colander. Cut the flesh into 2 cm (¾ in) chunks and add to a blender.

Heat a saucepan of water until very small bubbles start to appear on the base of the pan, indicating the water is around 70°C (158°F), or use a cooking thermometer to check. If you add a knotted pandan leaf while heating the water, this will give an added perfume to your final coconut cream – a nice addition, but certainly not essential. Add enough water to the food processor to completely cover the coconut flesh chunks.

Blend the coconut flesh with the water for a few minutes until it is a very fine, soft and wet textured pulpy mass. Blend for longer if necessary, as the finer the pulp, the easier it will be to achieve a greater yield later.

Transfer the pulp to a clean tea towel (dish towel) or muslin (cheesecloth), then gather the edges and squeeze the pulp of all its liquid into a glass or plastic container (never metal, as this can taint the cream). Leave the liquid for 30 minutes or longer to separate. The thicker coconut cream will float to the surface of the thinner, slightly opaque coconut milk. Once fully separated, you can use a ladle to skim off the top layer of coconut cream. Do not discard the thinner milk, as this can also be used in your cooking to braise and poach vegetables, or as a thin coconut stock to moisten curries and soups. It is also worth noting that the resulting dry coconut pulp from the squeezing process can be repurposed and used as a smoking agent for when you next have a barbecue (see method below).

Both the cream and milk are best used on the same day; any longer and they risk spoiling. If kept overnight, then refrigerate both, but it should be noted that this process will harden and solidify the cream, making it harder to use. If you are left with excess coconut cream, then a useful process is to 'crack' or split the cream; a technique that involves simmering the cream until most of its water content has been evaporated, resulting in curdled cream solids with an oily surface. This 'cracked' cream is especially useful for frying out curry pastes, and has an almost indefinite shelf life once stored in the refrigerator or freezer (more on the separating method below).

Separating coconut cream

MAKES 150 G (5 OZ)

400g (14 oz) thickest coconut cream (the richer, heavier solids that rise to the surface of the thinner milk)
1 tablespoon coconut oil (if using shop-bought coconut cream)

Warm the coconut cream in a saucepan over a low–medium heat for 5 minutes until the cream starts to simmer. Continue to cook the cream while stirring frequently, until it begins to thicken and 'crack' or separate. Cook for a further 3–5 minutes until the cream separates, the thinner liquid evaporates, and the surface develops an oily sheen. If using shop-bought coconut cream, add 1–2 tablespoons of coconut oil to the cream as you are simmering it to facilitate the process. This is because shop-bought cream has been homogenised and stabilised, making the separating process almost impossible without adding the oil. Leave the 'cracked' cream to cool before storing indefinitely in the refrigerator or freezer.

Coconut smoke mix

MAKES 400 G (14 OZ)

200 g (7 oz/1 cup) rice
2 fresh pandan leaves, thinly sliced lengthways (omit if not available)
200 g (7 oz) squeezed pulp from making coconut cream

Soak the rice in a bowl of water for 30 minutes, then drain well with a sieve (fine-mesh strainer). In a bowl, combine the pandan leaves, squeezed coconut pulp and drained rice. Sprinkle this mixture over hot coals to produce a coconut-scented smoke when barbecuing (grilling) meats and seafood. The mix can be stored in the refrigerator for 2–3 days or portioned for use straight from the freezer.

hom jiaw/nahm man hom

Fried Shallots and Fragrant Shallot Oil

Golden-brown, crispy fried shallots are used throughout Thailand to give depth of flavour, sweetness and texture to all manner of dishes, from soups and salads to curries and stir-fries. There is rarely a dish that doesn't improve with a scattering of fried shallots tossed through. The process involves deep-frying thinly sliced shallots in oil until they lose their water content, becoming crispy, fragrant and golden brown. You can do this using any fat of your choice, but I opt for a neutral-tasting vegetable oil, as the frying process imparts a wonderful flavour to the oil, making it a superior cooking oil for other dishes like stir-fries and curries, or just for use as a fragrant shallot oil to drizzle over fried rice and soups. Fried shallots can be bought from supermarkets (grocery stores), as a sort of hot dog-style crunchy garnish, but nothing beats shallots that you have fried yourself.

MAKES 100 G (3½ OZ)

200 g (7 oz) shallots, peeled (small round or banana shallots work best, but they must be very fresh and firm)

500 ml (17 fl oz/2 cups) vegetable oil

Halve the shallots lengthways, then slice them as thinly as you can with the grain of the shallot, aiming for slices 1 mm (1/32 in) thick. Take your time, as you are looking for a uniform thickness so that the shallots fry evenly. Using a Japanese mandolin makes the job easier.

Line a large baking tray (pan) with paper towels. Heat the vegetable oil in a large wok until it reaches 140°C (284°F) on a cooking thermometer. If you don't own one, add a slice of shallot to the hot oil; if it starts to bubble and fry without taking on colour immediately, the temperature is correct.

Add the remaining shallots to the hot oil and stir to prevent them clumping together. Maintain a steady oil temperature so that the shallots are kept at a gentle sizzle for about 12 minutes, or until they turn golden brown.

Strain the shallots through a sieve (fine-mesh strainer) over a heatproof dish so that the oil is collected. Shake the sieve, then transfer the shallots to the lined tray. Use two forks to gently tease the shallots apart into strands, separating them into a single layer on the paper. The shallots will darken and become crispier as they dry. You want them to dry and cool as quickly as possible to prevent them turning too dark and becoming bitter. This takes some practice, but you will quickly realise how dark you want the shallots to be before straining.

Leave the fried shallots to cool completely before storing in an airtight container lined with a sheet of paper towel. Store in a cool dry place for up to two weeks. Leave the fragrant shallot oil to cool completely before transferring to a separate airtight container. It will keep in a cool, dry place for up to two months.

gratiam jiaw/nahm man gratiam

Fried Garlic and Fragrant Garlic Oil

Much like fried shallots, crispy fried nibs of garlic improve most dishes, providing an almost nutty richness. Something as simple as steamed rice topped with fried garlic can become an addictive snack. I add a sprinkle to minced (ground) meat (*laabs*) and salads, particularly those originating from Northern Thailand. The fragrant garlic oil gives wonderful flavour when drizzled over soups and broken rice porridge (*jok*).

MAKES 80 G (30 OZ)

160 g (5½ oz) garlic cloves, peeled and chopped
500 ml (17 fl oz/2 cups) vegetable oil

In a pestle and mortar, pound the garlic into a uniform minced texture, resembling a somewhat coarse paste. Do this in batches so as to not overcrowd the mortar. Alternatively, if you own a mincer (grinder), then mince (grind) the garlic through the smallest hole.

Line a large baking tray (pan) with paper towels. Heat the vegetable oil in a large wok until it reaches 140°C (284°F) on a cooking thermometer. If you don't own one, add a speck of very finely chopped garlic to the oil; if it starts to bubble and fry without taking on colour immediately, the temperature is correct.

Add the remaining garlic to the oil and stir to prevent it clumping together. Maintain a steady oil temperature so that the garlic is kept at a gentle sizzle for about 12 minutes, or until golden brown.

Strain the fried garlic through a sieve (fine-mesh strainer) over a heatproof dish so that the oil is collected. Shake the sieve, then transfer the fried garlic to the lined tray and spread it out in a thin single layer on the paper. The garlic will darken and become crispier as it dries. You want it to dry and cool as quickly as possible to prevent it turning too dark and becoming bitter. This takes some practice, but you will quickly realise how dark you want the garlic to be before straining.

Leave the fried garlic to cool completely before storing in an airtight container lined with a sheet of paper towel. Store in a cool dry place for up to two weeks. Leave the fragrant garlic oil to cool completely before transferring to a separate airtight container. It will keep in a cool, dry place for up to two months. Once the fried garlic and fragrant garlic oil are completely cooled, you can make a condiment by adding one part crispy fried garlic flakes to two parts fragrant oil. This is great for adding seasoning at the table to noodle soups, fried rice and rice porridge.

khao khua

Toasted Rice Powder

This is a storecupboard ingredient that's widely used in dishes throughout Isaan. The process showcases the resourcefulness of Thai cooks by essentially creating another ingredient from the rice grown in the poorer, rural areas of the country. Raw rice grains are dry-toasted over a low heat, giving a nutty and roasted flavour. Once ground into a powder, this provides texture, crunch and a subtle smoky flavour to dishes. Traditionally this is done using sticky rice, which is grown abundantly in Isaan, but I have tested the process with jasmine rice, wild rice and even British grains such as pearl barley with great success.

MAKES 100 G (3½ OZ)

100 g (3½ oz/½ cup) uncooked sticky rice
4 outer husks of lemongrass, chopped (optional)
2 makrut lime leaves (fresh or frozen) (optional)

Dry-toast the uncooked rice with the lemongrass husks and makrut lime leaves in a wok or heavy-based pan over a low heat for 5 minutes, moving the rice constantly so that the grains turn a deep golden-brown colour and smell toasty and nutty.

Remove and discard the lemongrass and makrut lime leaves, then grind the toasted rice in a granite pestle and mortar to a somewhat coarse powder. Work in batches if necessary so as to not overcrowd the mortar. Alternatively, use a spice grinder or hand-held blender, but be careful not to overgrind the grains into too fine a powder. You are looking for a texture that resembles sand. Keep in an airtight container in a dark place for up to two weeks; any longer, and the rice will lose its aromatic fragrance.

prik bon

Toasted Chilli Powder

This condiment and seasoning powder is beloved throughout Thailand for flavouring salad dressings, dipping sauces, soups, stir-fries and curries. Thai's love for *prik bon* is so ingrained in their eating culture that this ubiquitous toasted chilli powder is found on all dining tables, from homes to street-food vendors and restaurants. Shop-bought crushed dried chilli flakes or chilli powder are fine to use, but you won't get the same depth of flavour as you do when you dry-toast the chillies yourself until blistered, smoky and charred.

MAKES 200 G (7 OZ)

200 g (7 oz) dried long red chillies, seeded
25 g (1 oz) dried bird's eye chillies

Dry-toast the dried long red chillies in a wok over a medium heat for 10 minutes, moving them around frequently so that the chillies colour evenly and darken. Some black blistering and charring is good for flavour, but too much will cause the final chilli powder to become dark and bitter. Remove from the wok and repeat the process for the bird's eye chillies, this time cooking for 5 minutes.

Blitz the chillies in a hand-held blender or spice grinder to a powder of your chosen texture. I prefer my *prik bon* with a little more texture than shop-bought chilli powder, more like that of sand. Be careful not to blitz any of the chilli seeds that have fallen out of the chillies and become burnt and blackened while toasting, as these will be bitter. Store in an airtight container away from direct sunlight for up to two months.

nahm makham piak
Tamarind Water

This simple preparation gives you a fruity sour liquid that can be used to season all kinds of Thai dishes, ranging from the very simple to the incredibly complex. I find the flavour reminiscent of tart plums and sweet dates, to give you an idea of the taste. Ready-made pots of tamarind concentrate are available to buy in Asian supermarkets (grocery stores), and I must admit I keep a pot in the refrigerator for emergencies, but the flavour doesn't compare to tamarind water freshly made from the sticky and fibrous paste. It can be made ahead of time and will keep well in the refrigerator for a week, but any longer and the water will start to ferment. Look for Thai brands and avoid any that have sugars or other added ingredients. You want 100 per cent tamarind pulp and flavour.

MAKES 400 G (14 OZ)

4 tablespoons (60 g/2 oz)
  tamarind pulp
550 ml (18½ fl oz/scant 2½ cups)
  warm water

Break up the tamarind pulp in a bowl, then pour over the warm water. Use your hands to mash and break the pulp further so that it becomes a thick liquid. Leave to stand for 15 minutes for the pulp to loosen with the water.

Pour the liquid through a sieve (fine-mesh strainer), using the back of a spatula or wooden spoon to press and scrape the pulp, extracting the thick tamarind purée. If the fibrous pulp looks as though it still has plenty of tamarind flesh attached to it then repeat this soaking and straining process, but this time use caution and only add enough water to just cover the pulp, mashing well with your hands to release all the remaining flesh.

Discard the fibrous pulp and stones (pits). Stir the collected purée to completely incorporate the water. You want this to be quite thick and very sour, as it can always be diluted to the desired thickness and sourness later. When using in a more diluted state, remember that it will ultimately dilute the dish you are seasoning, be that a curry, soup or salad, so use your intuition and keep this base thick and powerful in flavour. The tamarind water will keep in an airtight container in the refrigerator for up to a week, or can be frozen in portions for up to three months.

nahm pla raa

Fermented Fish Sauce

This seasoning sauce is used throughout Thailand, particularly in the Northeastern (Isaan) region of the country, where its pungency can be detected in nearly every dish, from salads to soups and curries. Fermented fish is made by salting freshwater fish before mixing with rice bran and fermenting for at least eight months until the desired flavour and consistency is achieved. Thai cooks will wrap the fermented fish fillets in banana leaf and grill them briefly to release their pungent flavours before adding to dishes. In extreme circumstances, the grilled fermented fish is eaten simply with rice and a squeeze of lime juice. I prefer to buy glass jars of the whole fillets as opposed to the finished seasoning sauce so that I can 'cook out' the fillets with aromatic ingredients to soften the flavour and pasteurise the sauce before using. There are a few brands available, but I recommend Thai brand Pantainorasingh (Pantai) as it doesn't contain any hidden sugars and seasonings. It's sometimes sold as 'pickled gouramy fish sauce'.

MAKES 300 G (10½ OZ)

454 g (1 lb) jar pickled gouramy fish fillets (fermented fish sauce)
650 ml (22 fl oz/generous 2¾ cups) water
1 ripe pineapple core, chopped
roots and outer husks of 8 lemongrass stalks, chopped
8 makrut lime leaves (fresh or frozen)
5 cm (2 in) piece of galangal, peeled and chopped
3 tablespoons chopped banana shallot
2 tablespoons garlic cloves, bruised
2 tablespoons chopped coriander (cilantro) root or coriander stem
1½ tablespoons palm or brown sugar
1 pandan leaf, knotted

Combine the pickled gouramy fish fillets and water in a large saucepan and warm gently over a low heat, stirring to dissolve the fish with the water.

Add the remaining ingredients and simmer over a very low heat for 5–10 minutes. If it looks too thick, then add more water as necessary. It should be a pouring consistency.

Remove from the heat and leave to stand for 30 minutes for the flavours of the aromatic ingredients to infuse. Pass through a sieve (fine-mesh strainer), pressing the fermented fish sauce with the back of a spoon to extract the maximum flavour and discarding the solid ingredients. Leave to cool completely before transferring to an airtight container and storing in the refrigerator for up to 2 weeks, or portion and freeze for up to six months.

nahm man
Rendered Animal Fat

Animal fat, particularly pork, is the traditional cooking fat of Thailand. It gives body and richness to dishes from the very beginning of their story. However, it also comes with added cholesterol, and because of this vegetable oil is now more commonly used in modern Thai cooking. I personally like to use animal fats for some recipes, as I feel the results are far superior. I also include these instructions as it's good practice to use an animal in its entirety, and if you're left with excess fat it can be rendered to use throughout other dishes. Rendered animal fat freezes well, so it doesn't have to be used immediately; instead, it can be saved for those dishes that particularly benefit from the added richness.

MAKES 300–400 G (10½–14 OZ)

500 g (1 lb 2 oz) animal fat (this can be anything, from pork, beef or lamb, to duck and chicken)
3 tablespoons water
2 tablespoons chopped coriander (cilantro) root or coriander stem
3 tablespoons chopped ginger root
3 tablespoons chopped garlic
½ teaspoon salt
¼ teaspoon white peppercorns

Finely chop the animal fat or, if buying fat for this purpose, then you can ask your butcher to mince (grind) the fat for you.

Add the chopped or minced fat to a large saucepan with the water and warm over a low heat for 15–20 minutes until the fat renders and the water evaporates. Stir frequently to ensure the pieces of fat don't stick to the base of the pan. The fat will begin to colour and turn crispy; you want the pieces to turn a lovely golden brown and become very crispy, indicating there is no more water left in them. Meanwhile, in a pestle and mortar, pound the coriander root, ginger, garlic, salt and peppercorns to a fine paste. Once the fat is almost completely rendered, carefully add the paste and stir well with the rendered fat. The paste will fizzle and give off a lovely fragrance as it fries. Once the paste is golden and crispy like the rendered fat pieces, pour the contents through a sieve (fine-mesh strainer) into a heatproof bowl.

Leave the liquid fat to cool to room temperature before storing in an airtight container in the refrigerator for up to a month, or you can freeze it for up to six months. The crispy fried scratchings and garlic paste can be used to add crunch to salads or for topping stir-fries and relishes, but they will only remain crispy and delicious for a day or two, so use immediately, if at all.

prik nahm pla

Chillies Soaked in Fish Sauce

This is the ultimate Thai condiment. It's salty and hot, providing a flavour boost and instant spice upgrade to any dish – I smother it on every mouthful of fried rice and stir-fried noodles! Ratios are all down to personal preference. I use fistfuls of fresh chillies in my recipe, but you may prefer to tread on the side of caution.

MAKES 120 G (4 OZ)

8 bird's eye chillies, chopped
1 garlic clove, very finely chopped
6 tablespoons fish sauce
1 tablespoon lime juice

Add all the ingredients to a small bowl and mix to combine.

Leave to stand for at least 30 minutes before using to allow the flavours to meld together. You can keep this in the refrigerator for several days, but my personal preference is to make it as and when you require it.

When using, scoop out the desired amount of soaked chillies and garlic to slather over your food, or drizzle over the *slightly* less intense liquid to give a boost of seasoning.

nahm jim jaew Isaan

Chilli and Tamarind Sauce

This is a super-versatile dipping sauce that complements any kind of grilled or smoked meat, particularly Grilled Coriander and Garlic Chicken (*gai yang*) (page 64) or simply a steak that's been rolled in fish sauce before hitting the hot grill. This recipe is based on similar *jaew* dipping sauces found throughout Isaan.

This style of *jaew* is commonly served with finely sliced lemongrass, chopped herbs (such as coriander (cilantro), sawtooth coriander, hot mint and dill), and toasted rice powder stirred through it. This should be done at the last minute, as the herbs and rice powder will soften and lose their appeal after an hour. Add a squeeze of fresh lime juice to the *jaew* before serving to brighten the flavours.

MAKES 650 G (1 LB 7 OZ)

200 g (7 oz/generous 1 cup) palm sugar
3 tablespoons water
240 ml (8¼ fl oz/generous 1 cup) Tamarind Water (*nahm makham piak*) (page 214)
200 ml (7 fl oz/scant 1 cup) fish sauce
2 tablespoons Toasted Chilli Powder (*prik bon*) (page 213)

Break the palm sugar into small pieces and add to a saucepan with the water. Very gently heat for 3 minutes until the sugar has dissolved. You are effectively making a palm sugar syrup. Leave to cool to room temperature.

Add the remaining ingredients to the palm sugar syrup and whisk together to combine. Use immediately or store in the refrigerator in an airtight container for up to a week.

nahm jim gai waan

Sweet Chilli Sauce

Thai sweet chilli sauce has become a supermarket (grocery store) shelf staple, but like most foreign condiments adopted into the Western repertoire, it has been warped into something unrecognisable from the original. There is no getting away from the fact the sauce is sweet (after all, it's in the name) but this version provides balance through acidity and heat, which is a welcome change from the gluey sauces many will have sitting in their kitchen cupboard. This goes particularly well with Grilled Coriander and Garlic Chicken (*gai yang*) (page 64) and Fish Cakes with Cucumber Pickle (*tort man pla*) (page 120).

MAKES 550 G (1 LB 2 OZ)

180 g (6 oz/¾ cup) caster (superfine) sugar
120 ml (4 fl oz/½ cup) white wine vinegar
120 ml (4 fl oz/½ cup) water
5 long red chillies, seeded and chopped
3 red bird's eye chillies, chopped
2 tablespoons chopped garlic
1 teaspoon salt

Combine the sugar, vinegar and water in a medium saucepan and warm over a medium heat to dissolve the sugar for 3 minutes. Once fully dissolved, simmer for a further 5 minutes.

In a pestle and mortar, pound the chillies, garlic and salt to a smooth paste, then add this to the pan. Whisk to combine, then simmer for another 5 minutes, or until the mixture is reduced to a light syrup. Remember the sauce will continue to thicken as it cools.

Leave to cool to room temperature before using, or store in an airtight container in the refrigerator for up to two months.

prik dong nahm som

Fermented Chilli Vinegar

This is an intensely spicy and sour chilli sauce that is best eaten with fatty dishes to help cut through the richness and provide balance. The sauce is great on its own, but feel free to use it as a base by adding additional sugar, salt or vinegar to tweak to your own personal preference based on the dish you are serving it alongside.

MAKES 200 G (7 OZ)

4 long red chillies, seeded
3 red bird's eye chillies
2 tablespoons garlic, peeled
4 tablespoons caster (superfine) sugar
100 ml (3½ fl oz/scant ½ cup) distilled white rice vinegar
salt

Have a large bowl filled with iced water ready nearby. Bring a large saucepan of water to the boil and season with salt. Add the chillies and garlic to the boiling water and blanch for 2 minutes. Refresh in the iced water and drain well, then roughly chop.

In a pestle and mortar, pound the chillies, garlic and 1 tablespoon salt until smooth. Add the sugar and vinegar and mix to ensure the sugar is completely dissolved. It will taste very spicy and sour with a background sweetness to balance the intense flavours.

Transfer to an airtight container and leave at room temperature for three days to allow the chillies to ferment and become naturally sour. Transfer to the refrigerator, where the sauce will keep almost indefinitely. For the best results, leave for five days in the refrigerator before using to allow the flavours to suitably develop.

nahm jim dtow jiaw

Yellow Soybean, Ginger and Elderflower Sauce

This sauce is a riff on those served by street vendors selling Hainanese chicken over rice (*khao man gai*), but I find it pairs well with smoked chicken or grilled white fish. During the summer months, I forage for elderflowers to create elderflower-infused vinegar, which I use to season dishes, giving them a lovely floral and quintessentially British flavour. This recipe works particularly well with elderflower vinegar, but you can also use ordinary white vinegar.

MAKES 570 G (1 LB 4OZ)

2 tablespoons chopped coriander (cilantro) root or coriander stem
4 tablespoons chopped garlic
4½ tablespoons chopped ginger root
1 tablespoon chopped red bird's eye chillies
1 teaspoon salt
½ teaspoon white peppercorns
3 tablespoons palm sugar
325 g (11½ oz) yellow soybean sauce
200 ml (7 fl oz/scant 1 cup) elderflower vinegar or white wine vinegar

In a pestle and mortar, pound the coriander root, garlic, ginger and chillies with the salt and white pepper to form a smooth paste. Add the sugar and pound again to a smooth paste.

Add the yellow soybean sauce and vinegar, then mix everything together well. It will taste umami and salty, with a background heat from the chillies, ginger and garlic, while being slightly sweet and sour with a floral elderflower finish. Store in an airtight container in the refrigerator for up to two weeks.

About the Author

Acknowledgements

John Chantarasak is a half-Thai, half-British chef based in London. Having grown up in Wales while regularly travelling to his father's native Thailand, the food John cooks today has been influenced by his experiences of both Thailand and the UK. After training at Le Cordon Bleu in Bangkok, John worked in the kitchens of David Thompson, whose restaurant Nahm is one of the most highly regarded Thai restaurants in the world. John's reputation has grown through numerous sell-out pop-ups and residencies across the UK, Europe, North America and Southeast Asia, making seats for his events some of the most sought after in the country.

John's focus is now on his London-based restaurant, AngloThai, which he runs with his wife Desiree.

Dedicated to my Desiree and Rufus, the loves of my life. Without them I would not be the person I am today.

Thanks to my parents, Don and Lisa, for giving me the foundations of life and teaching me to be a better person each and every day. Big love to my brother and sister, Nick and Sam, for always inspiring me with their love and friendship. Shout outs to Jonty, Anna and Caspar, and all my wider family!

Pete and Sue for putting a roof over my head during lockdown 2.0 and giving me the support to write this cookbook and with every other aspect of life.

Ben Baptie – my best mate to the end.

Too many friends and loved ones to mention, but a handful of special thanks to Nicholas Balfe – the OG AngloThai brother, top breddos Nud and Chris, Adam Heanen and the whole HG Walter family, Jack and Ronnie, the Liverpool Belzan massive (Sam, Chris and Owain), Abby and Luke, Brad and Holly, Lee Westcott, Will Bowlby, Big D, Nic Rizzi, Clerkenwell Tim, Jake and Marco, Lee Tiernan and BAM, Ben Broomfield, Debs Crowshaw, all past and present P. Franco legends, plus Andy Oliver and all the 'golden era' Som Saa team – you know who you are!

Everyone that I've cooked with through the years, thank you for making me most welcome and giving me a platform to showcase my cooking.

Kim Hillyard for painting the artwork for this book and for all your other amazing work to date that has given AngloThai a visual identity through colours and shapes.

Hardie Grant for believing in me to write this cookbook. Eve for making it all happen and Kate for constantly dealing with my bullshit and weirdness. Maureen for capturing such beautiful images and Alex for your wonderful styling.

To the people of Thailand for your beautiful country, cuisine and culture.

Finally, to everyone that has been a customer at AngloThai – your support does not go unnoticed and I can't thank you all enough for the constant support.

Index

Published in 2022 by Hardie Grant Books,
an imprint of Hardie Grant Publishing

Hardie Grant Books (London)
5th & 6th Floors
52–54 Southwark Street
London SE1 1UN

Hardie Grant Books (Melbourne)
Building 1, 658 Church Street
Richmond, Victoria 3121

hardiegrantbooks.com

British Library Cataloguing-in-Publication Data. A catalogue
record for this book is available from the British Library.

Kin Thai
ISBN: 9781784884802

10 9 8 7 6 5 4 3 2 1

Publisher: Kajal Mistry
Commissioning Editor: Eve Marleau
Project Editor: Kate Burkett
Design and Art Direction: Daniel New
Illustrations: Kim Hillyard
Photographer: Maureen M. Evans
Food Assistant: Kim Ratcharoen
Prop Stylist: Alexander Breeze
Copy-editor: Kathy Steer
Proofreader: Tara O' Sullivan
Indexer: Cathy Heath
Production Controller: Katie Jarvis

Colour reproduction by p2d
Printed and bound in China by Leo Paper Products Ltd.